OFFICIAL TRUTH
101 PROOF

Da Capo Press

A Member of the Perseus Books Group

REX BROWN

OFFICIAL TRUTH

THE INSIDE
STORY OF
PANTERA

101 PROOF

WITH MARK EGLINTON

781.66092
PAN

Editorial production by *Marra*thon Production services. www.marrathon.net

Design by Jane Raese
Set in 12-point Dante

Library of Congress Cataloging-in-Publication Data is available for this book.
ISBN 978-0-306-82137-0
ISBN 978-0-306-82138-7 (e-Book)

First Da Capo Press edition 2013

Da Capo Press books are available at special discounts for bulk purchases in the U.S. by corporations, institutions, and other organizations. For more information, please contact the Special Markets Department at the Perseus Books Group, 2300 Chestnut Street, Suite 200, Philadelphia, PA 19103, or call (800) 810-4145, ext. 5000, or e-mail special.markets@perseusbooks.com.

10 9 8 7 6 5 4 3 2 1

THIS WOULD NOT HAVE BEEN POSSIBLE WITHOUT
YOUR SCREAMS & ADULATIONS, MANY, IN FACT!!!

LOVE YOU ALL, REX

CONTENTS

PROLOGUE   xi

1   HEADS UP   1

2   DADDY BILL   9

3   ON DOWN THE LINE   19

4   REX, DRUGS, AND ROCK 'N' ROLL   29

5   12 O'CLOCK HIGH   39

6   THE KID FROM THE BIG EASY   55

7   WE'RE TAKING OVER THIS TOWN   63

8   EARLY TOURS AND ANECDOTES   75

9   DANGEROUSLY VULGAR   85

10   CONTROLLED CHAOS   101

11   YOU FAT BASTARD!   109

12   GOING DEEP, HEAD FIRST   131

13   *TRENDKILL* OUT ON THE TILES   139

14   THE 'TUDE   159

15   SABBATH AND DOWN WITH THE GAMBLER   167

16   SWAN SONG   177

17   THE DOWNFALL!!   187

18   LOST LOVE AND THIRTY DAYS IN THE HOLE   203

19   THE WORST DAY OF MY LIFE   215

20   THE AFTERMATH   223

21   THE HOLLYWOOD EXPERIMENT   229

22   SEVEN 'TIL SEVEN NO ONE KNOWS WHAT
     WILL HAPPEN   241

     A WORD FROM THE AUTHOR   247

     A NOTE FROM THE CO-AUTHOR   249

     ACKNOWLEDGMENTS   251

     REX BROWN COMPLETE DISCOGRAPHY   257

I remember back in '87 when Pantera and King's X did a double in-store together in Dallas. Both our bands pretty much kept to ourselves, but all I remember was that Dime was in the corner shredding through a very loud amp practically the whole time, with a bunch of wide-open metalheads going nuts. He was simply fucking amazing!

Fast-forward two years. Pantera played the Backstage Club in Houston (a real cool club that everyone played), and me and my buds Galactic Cowboys went to check them out. Well, I wish everyone could have been there to see them that night doing *Power Metal*. It was the tightest, most brutal metal I had ever heard in my entire life. Phil, Vinnie, and Dime were mesmerizing, but me being a bass player, I completely focused on Rex. In my opinion, Rex is not only the coolest looking bass player ever, but he could execute every song with the kind of brutality and groove that was rocking me like only a bass player can, and holding down the fort.

Oh, and also they did some amazing Metallica covers. Pantera executed every song with a power on a level I had never experienced before. We hung out back stage drinking and having fun. This became the norm, but on one particular night they came to play, everyone was there, ready to experience this sound we had so gotten addicted to and loved so much. To our surprise, they did a whole set of new songs. It was the entire *Cowboys from Hell* album. All I can remember is that there was an amazing vibe that we all had just experienced the future of Metal. The rest is history.

—dUg Pinnick, Kings X

PROLOGUE

"DIME, I CAN'T HANDLE YOUR FUCKING BROTHER."

Those were some of the first words that came out of my mouth when communication between Dime and me resumed sometime in late 2003. Any previous contact we'd had had been strained for sure, and this was hardly a friendly greeting, I know, but I was tired of all of Vinnie's bullshit, tired of trying to coordinate tours around his titty-bar escapades, and I definitely didn't like the fact that Dime's brother was drawing all kinds of negative attention on the rest of the band with his childish actions. It was all just fucking mindless horse-shit, and after years of keeping quiet—although the fact that I switched buses on one of the last tours to escape all the nonsense should have been an obvious indication of my unhappiness—I needed Dime to know how I felt, and that we should all do some se-rious thinking before we even considered continuing to be a band.

From where Dime was sitting, I'm sure he felt that Phil and I had walked away from Pantera because we had taken 2002 off from the band to do the second Down record. We planned to go and tour the Down record for a bit, sure, and then the offer came to take part in Ozzfest 2002 as main headliners on the second stage—something we obviously couldn't turn down. So those are the facts as to why things turned out like they did. The bottom line is this: Vinnie and Dime had a problem with Phil and me being in Down, and I was the one they went through to bitch about it.

All through 2003 relations were very strained because of Philip's inability to answer the fucking phone—not for the first time or the last—to discuss what the future held for Pantera. Neither management nor I could even talk to him, far less the brothers, who were scared to death to even dial his number. So when we eventually got confirmation that Phil was doing his Superjoint Ritual project that year, we were all left in limbo.

Dime and I talked again on July 27, 2004, my fortieth birthday. My wife had made an effort and asked Dime to come along to a surprise party for me, but unfortunately he was out of town at the time so couldn't make it. It seemed like a phone call was the best I was going to get. "Don't expect me take you out and treat you to a steak dinner or anything like that," he told me, as if to say that he owed me nothing.

! ＃ ⊕ *

AS 2004 PASSED, our contact drifted to the point that, by the time we spoke again in November, it felt like Dime had become some kind of estranged brother. Again, we discussed all aspects of the band and the reasons why communication had broken down, and we both acknowledged that we needed some time apart from each other. It was a very emotional conversation, and when I hung up the phone I cried my eyeballs out because I missed him so much. But despite my sadness I always truly believed that all our differences would be worked out in time and that Pantera would continue. It just felt like when brothers fight and don't talk for a while, that's what brothers do. Despite how upsetting the awkwardness was, I never saw it as a permanent communication breakdown.

At this stage, Philip was completely out of the picture. He was still doped out of his mind and I had decided that there was no possibility of working with him again until his addiction situation changed. It is one thing trying to reason with someone who simply drinks and has a good time, but it's an entirely different matter when you're trying to reason with someone who's using—they're on a different fucking planet. Thank God he's got his life together now.

But as soon as he got his shit together—which I knew he eventually would—we could at least sit in the same room again and work out our differences. But I also understood that any reunion that could occur would require a great deal of structure, and there was no doubt in my mind that the task of putting it all in place would eventually fall on my plate. I felt caught in the middle fucking big time. Worse than that, it really pissed me off that I was the one getting emails from Vinnie every day—every single fucking day, saying, "Philip said this, Philip said that" and then having to listen to Vinnie whining about everything; on top of all that, reading Blabbermouth—a metal gossip site with a particularly vicious asshole group of commenters who put their own dramatic spin on every word spoken. Eventually I just got to the point where I simply didn't give a fuck anymore.

On the night of the shooting—December 8, 2004, as if I could forget—I was at home. I was originally intending on heading to Dallas to a Marilyn Manson show because our tour manager, Guy Sykes, was working for him by this time, and I planned to hang out with him for the night. I'd been saucing all day long, playing golf and the whole bit, and a few friends unrelated to the band ended up back at my house.

Then the phone rang.

It was around 10:00 p.m. and it was Kate Richardson, Phil Anselmo's girlfriend, on the line. We were chatting for a while when suddenly she got a phone call on another line, and then, when she returned to me, her tone had changed. She told me to put the television on, which I immediately did.

I couldn't believe what I was witnessing. Police sirens. Ambulances. Panic in Columbus, Ohio. Dime—our brother—murdered *on stage*? Dead? Dime? The images on the screen just fucking floored me. On the tiles. Straight up.

Although I had been drinking, I sobered up real fast. It was the only way I could hope to process what I was seeing. By now the news was all over CNN and every other news channel. Friends and family, who were also catching the news, began calling before I could even come to terms with the devastation that I felt, all wanting to know that I was okay. Guy Sykes left the Manson show in town and immediately made a beeline for my house. I was so shocked that I didn't even know what to think, let alone say, and phone calls just kept coming on the two landlines and four separate cell phones we had in the house, until I eventually fell asleep, probably as the sun was coming up.

"RITA WANTS YOU over at the house."

The following day, Guy Sykes's phone call confirmed that Dime's wife wanted to see me, so I headed over to her place only to find a bunch of fucking assholes hanging around. These were some of the parasitic hangers-on that Dime had accumulated over years of partying with fans and there were a few venomous looks and snide remarks aimed in my direction, but I ignored them all. I can only assume that some of these people saw my alliance with Philip as being disloyal to Dime and wanted to make me feel guilty for what had happened. Because these assholes had been following the whole thing in the press, it felt like there was already tension in the air, as if there had been an imaginary line drawn in the sand as to who was taking what side.

One of the security guys even squared up to me and tried to block my path from entering. I had some previous history with this particular guy, too, and had actually knocked the goon's teeth out acciden-tally on an earlier occasion. He'd even tried to sue me, unsuccessfully, so I certainly wasn't afraid of his posturing now and walked by him like he wasn't there.

Meanwhile various friends of Dime's and musicians from all kinds of other bands had already started to come in to town, and most of them were at the Wyndham Arlington South hotel and in a collective state of disbelief that Dime—the most fan-friendly of all dudes—could have been killed by a fan. The irony was just unfathomable. A lot of these people hadn't been in the same room together for years, so while the reason for being there was truly awful, there did seem to be a collective sense of solidarity that was celebratory and almost uplifting, which is something that Dime would have appreciated.

Back at Rita's house with Dime's close family, the mood was con-siderably more tense. As if to add to the uneasiness, Philip called from New Orleans to offer Rita his condolences, but when I passed the phone to her—at his request—she grabbed it angrily from me.

"If you even come close to Texas, I'll fucking shoot your ass," Rita told Philip, letting him know that she felt he had a role in the whole chain of events. His unsavory comments in the music press earlier that month were a big issue: "Dime deserves to be severely beaten"—comments he suggested were taken out of context, but no matter what he claims, I have the tapes of the interview in question, so I know *exactly* what he said. Phil and I seemed to have been put in the same camp, the only difference being that he was completely un-wanted and unwelcome, while I was just not the most popular guy around at that time. There was a difference.

The next day—still in a state of shock—Dime's dad Jerry, Vinnie, Rita, and I went to the Moore Funeral Home on North Davis Drive in Arlington, and there we saw the body of Darrell Abbott lying in a casket. For me, this was just too much. I had been to way too many funerals here—my mom, my grandmother, my dad—all of them ended up in this same room, but this particular one just shook me down to the core.

"See what you did?!!!" Vinnie Paul said to me, making the strange accusation that I was somehow responsible for Dime's death, which is obviously ridiculous. I had no idea how to reply to that, so I didn't.

"Is it okay that I'm here?" I asked Vince at a later point, making it clear that I didn't want to step on anyone's shoes in such a traumatic situation. I needed to check with him that all was cool.

"Of course," he said very definitively, making me wonder why he'd said what he did earlier. In my own head I couldn't stop myself from analyzing why Vinnie felt the way he did, and I just couldn't see why he would blame me for anything. Yes, the murderer who shot Dime was clearly mentally ill, but in my opinion the music press had been pushing all the wrong buttons with fans by constantly re-igniting the debate as to who was responsible for the break-up of Pantera. Since that point, I had talked to the police in Columbus and it was clear the incident wasn't only about Dime, it was about the whole band; so if Down had been in Columbus that night and not Damageplan, it could have been Phil or me who'd been killed instead.

If the press had shut their fuckin' mouths and let us—the band—resolve our differences, I believe that Darrell *would* still be alive today. The killer must not have been able to deal with the fact that Pantera had split up, so he decided to take his anger out on us, and he also had somehow in his delusion convinced himself that he had written our songs. He obviously had read the continuous press speculation and that, combined with his fragile state of mind, proved to be a fatal cocktail. After all, he had turned up at an earlier Damageplan show and torn up some gear before getting his ass kicked by security and thrown in jail, so he was already on the radar before that night in Columbus.

The following evening I got a phone call from Rita, and she asked me to be one of Dime's pallbearers and of course I agreed. It would have seemed disrespectful not to, but even still I couldn't help notice the glaring contradictions. Vinnie seemed to be blaming me in part for his brother's death, while at the same time Rita was asking me to perform an official duty. It just didn't make sense.

On the day of the funeral I didn't know what I was doing, who I was, or where I was—and that's no exaggeration. Unless you've ever been in a situation like this you can't understand. I had a couple of shots of whiskey—I simply had to or else I just could not have gotten through the day—and headed over to Rita's house again, very early, where there were more people than on the previous visit, guys like Zakk Wylde, Kat Brooks, and Pantera's sound guy Aaron Barnes, with whom I later rode in the same car to the funeral home. Everyone was just hanging out and trying to offer Rita as much support as possible.

"Let's do a shot for Dime!" someone shouted. This wouldn't be the only time these words would be heard over the next few days and consequently most people, myself included, seeking to ease the pain of what had happened, were at some level of inebriation throughout the funeral and memorial.

There were a huge number of Dime's musician friends there, and Eddie Van Halen and Zakk Wylde were asked to make speeches. I was sitting in the second row beside Eddie, who was just totally out of line, really disrespectful actually. I told Eddie on numerous occasions to shut the fuck up but there was no point. Zakk was always one of Dime's best friends, as well as being, like Dime, a great guitar player, but on this occasion he was in the bizarre situation of having to keep Eddie Van Halen—who was coked out of his head and acting like a complete idiot—in line.

"Fuckin' shut up," Zakk told Eddie after he had rambled on for a while while he was giving his eulogy—something about his ex-wife if I remember it right—but that didn't stop him, he just kept going. It was really disrespectful.

Despite the somber nature of the day, there was a danger of it becoming the "Eddie and Zakk Show" but thankfully it all calmed down. I was one of the last to go through and see Dime's body (my second time), and on this occasion I simply kissed him on the forehead. He was just so cold. *Right then* I emotionally checked out. Of course I was physically there, but mentally I was gone. I was just a shell and couldn't feel anything.

After the ceremony I went outside and lit a cigarette. I was shaking like a leaf. I wanted to get out of there and had a limousine waiting to do just that, but all I really wanted was my wife Belinda, who had come separately, to drive me home.

"Put me in the Hummer and just take me home," I told her.

And when I got there, I fell into a coma-like sleep. I didn't show up at the burial even though I was supposed to be a pallbearer. I just couldn't face it. I'm not even sure if anyone ever said anything about me not being there, but I wouldn't have cared if they had. Dime was the last person I wanted to put in the ground. I couldn't bear the thought of doing that to my best friend.

I woke at seven that evening to find my house full of people. I was persuaded to get up, get dressed, and of course have a shot or two for Dime. Our next destination was the Arlington Convention Center for Dime's public funeral service, and for some reason I was feeling uneasy, and up until the last minute wasn't sure that I was even going to go.

My uneasiness was entirely justified. Almost as soon as I walked into the venue, which was jammed with almost five thousand people, someone handed me yet another shot as I walked up toward the stage where Jerry Cantrell and his band were still playing. I was standing at the side, intently watching what was going on, and suddenly I was put on the spot. It was totally unexpected. There was this DJ guy there who had been given the role of official emcee, and I knew this clown from the past. He's one of those strip joint compere guys who introduces the girls in an overly dramatic way like, "Hey, on stage right now it's Ciiiinammmmooooooon!" or "Luscioussssssssssssss on stage three!" That's fine at a strip club—I would know—but I remember thinking that this guy being here wasn't just inappropriate, it was total fucking blasphemy and it seemed like the whole deal could turn into a fucking joke at any given second, if it hadn't already. Everything seemed to be disorganized and running behind schedule, but somehow Dime would have liked it that way as he once said—a little ironically, it turns out—that he'd even be late for his own funeral.

So, I was standing, watching, and suddenly this fucking DJ idiot put a microphone in my hand and asked me to say a few words to these five thousand or so people who were in attendance. Like I said, I didn't know I was going to be asked to say anything and I certainly didn't have a speech planned, so when I was up there I was desperately trying to find the words—any words—and in the end, all I could muster was "He loved you all. We'll miss him badly."

While this was happening, I was aware that this DJ idiot was pressurizing me all the time. "C'mon, Rex, we've got to go, we've got to go," is all I remember. Go where? Who the fuck knows, but after he said it, there were boos from the audience and in my numb state I wondered whether they were booing him or me. It was a really weird situation. In retrospect I think he was just trying to rush me off stage so they could get Vinnie up there. All I was trying to do was hold myself together that evening, and I wasn't doing that very well.

The whole place was a huge clusterfuck of security that night, with all kinds of barricades in place to keep certain people in certain designated areas. In my dazed headspace I decided I wanted to go down front-of-house, and on the way down the stairs I literally fell into the arms of Snake Sabo and Terry Date, who somehow managed to prop me up. They chaperoned me to the area I wanted to be in and put me in a seat between our manager Kim Zide and Charlie Benante. By then I was an emotional wreck and all Charlie could do was hold me like a baby.

One person obviously absent that day was Philip, although by this time he had flown into town—despite Rita's earlier warning—and was staying in a hotel, so I was phoning back and forth with him all day. I even went to see him for a while and kept him informed as to what was happening. I'm sure there was a part of him that wanted to be there—or at least be close to what was going on—but at the same time I'm certain he wanted to respect the family's wishes. Either way, it was a tough position for him, and one that would offer no closure whatsoever. The concept of him showing up unannounced would not have been well received given Rita's total insistence that he stay away.

So, frustrated by being excluded from all the events surrounding Dime's death, and cheated out of any closure on the death of one of his best friends and musical soul mates, Philip later wrote Vinnie a letter, but my suspicion is that it may not have been read or certainly not acknowledged in any way. It was suggested that Vinnie never even got it, but I'd bet that he did.

The days following the funeral were no less stressful. Every day my wife and me were harassed by reporters at our door—they even went through our trash and threw it all over the yard—trying to get any kind of comment from me about what had happened. I simply didn't want to get involved in any of that discussion because what else was there to say? So I just had my wife say to them, "He's not talking to anyone so you might as well fucking leave."

I went to the cemetery a few days later, alone. I wanted to say my own goodbyes to Darrell, but the public wouldn't even allow me this privacy with my friend, as I was continually harassed for comments and even autographs, all while I tried to spend a little private time at Dime's graveside. I remember this as one of the worst days of my life.

From that day on, I went into the "why?" loop, and I'm still asking the question. Maybe I always will be. I live with a constant combination of anger at the fucker who did this to my dear friend, and complete shock that the existence of the band with whom I'd spent my entire adult life has been ended by a series of events that were far beyond anyone's control. What you need to remember is that only four guys ever really knew what went on in Pantera, and one of us isn't around anymore to tell his side of the story.

OFFICIAL TRUTH
101 PROOF

CHAPTER 1

HEADS UP

If you put your head up above the fence often enough, eventually some fucker is going to throw a rock at you.

But when they stop throwing rocks, *that's* when you've really got a problem, because you're obviously not important any more. I have no clue whose quote that one up there in bold was—it might even be a combination of things a few people have said, but the message in there is that fame and fortune is truly a fucked-up concept. I mean, obviously it changes the way you dress and the way you present yourself in front of people, that's a given. But I found myself treating people differently, and not because of their personality or how they were to me. That didn't matter at all.

No, the reason was because I was in a higher tax bracket. Fuck, I'd sit there and say stupid shit like, "Dude, I've got more money than God." That must have sounded so arrogant and I'm embarrassed I ever said things like that. Sure, I liked the fame or, rather, aspects of the social acceptance that comes with it, but I liked the fortune better and I attribute that to having been brought up in a household where everything had been a struggle, particularly from a financial point of view. My conclusion, and I'm far from the first to say so, is that everything changes when money gets involved.

When you've been broke and solitary like I was as a teenager, barely cutting it, trying to make a two-hundred-buck-a-week salary cover the rent and still leave room to get a twelve-pack for the week or something like that, it's no surprise things get a little screwed when the checks start flying in, and then all you can say is, "What the fuck am I going to do with all this?!"

Well, what we did with it was spend it—too freely at times—but because we toured so much and accepted every good offer that was thrown our way, there always seemed to be a healthy cash flow to keep it all going. It felt great to finally have some money when I'd been poor all my life, I can't deny that. Do I wish I'd had a little more help at times, some wise and trustworthy financial advice? Of course I do, because I didn't really know how to go out there and invest, although I did do bonds but wished I hadn't once the stock market crashed on me. Eventually I learned how to save the money I was making, but there was a long learning curve.

What complicates things is that you've got money coming from so many different places: record royalties, tour money, merchandising, equipment endorsement deals . . . the list goes on, and all you can do is to trust somebody—in my case the company who was part of our business partnership—to pay all the bills and take care of all the taxes, so I really didn't have to worry about anything. I could just call them and say, "I need some money here, I need some money there" or whatever, or I could call and say, "Just cut a check for this to so and so" and they'd do it so I didn't have to. That left me to take care of the business I knew how to control: playing the music.

To have large amounts of cash at my disposal not only felt great, but it also balanced out all the sacrifices I'd made to get in this position: being on the road, being away from my family, and all the other difficulties that come from that kind of life.

Gradually though—and it doesn't matter a shit how much money you once had—you realize that not only do you *not* have more money than God, but you actually don't have nearly as much as you thought you did.

Then you panic and all you want to do is just *live*. I had gotten into the habit of living well—in a large house with every available comfort—and it was great for my kids to live in the type of environment where they can get anything they want, within reason. Being able to provide that meant a lot to me because it was the polar opposite to what it was like for me growing up. Remember, we were musicians, not accountants, and learning to look after your cash is something only learned after a lot of trial and error.

Meanwhile the other guys—Darrell and Vinnie most of all—were out spending a thousand dollars a night and then wondering where all the money went. I remember one day when Dime turned up at my front door out of the blue. I guess you could say I was like a father figure to him and he looked to me as some kind of source of wisdom. At least I think he did.

"Dude, I'm not sure but think I might be broke." Even the way he said it sounded idiotic.

Of course I said, "You might be broke? What does that even mean? What the fuck are you talking about, dude?"

"Well, I got into this investment thing with tanning beds and the whole bit and it hasn't worked out so well," Dime explained. Darrell had set up his girlfriend Rita Haney (she was his wife in every way except they never actually got married) in a tanning salon venture in an Arlington strip mall, and business hadn't been so good.

"Really? So aside from that, how much are you spending each night?" I asked him.

"I don't know—maybe a thousand dollars." (Trust me, that was the very least he would have been spending.)

"Okay, so if you've got three hundred grand in the bank, how many nights can you go out and spend that?" I said.

"Three thousand times?"

"Think again, buddy. Try three *hundred* times. No wonder you're fuckin' broke—you need to work on your math," I told him.

The sad truth is that Dime and Vinnie were out of control with their partying, and with nobody to keep them in line as they paraded themselves around Arlington with a growing bunch of hangers-on, cash would always run dry fast.

! # ⊕ *

AS FAME TOOK HOLD, we couldn't walk down the street without getting recognized by fans. I reverted to the quiet, unassuming approach that underpins my personality and started looking for little fuckin' dive watering holes to hang out and drink in without being harassed, somewhere close to the house so that I could get totally fucked up and get home quickly afterwards. Flying under the radar, you could say.

Even in interviews—a process I didn't really enjoy anyway—I just kept to myself. I'd show up of course but then I'd just sit there behind a pair of dark shades and not do a whole lot of anything. I wanted to try to keep my personal life separate from the band—which was impossible—and I also knew the other three guys would have plenty to say. I was always the quiet guy that nobody knew much about. I just liked to fucking jam, and that's the plain truth. If I'd wanted attention I would have had, like Vinnie, five bodyguards following me around.

I hated being asked the same questions all the time. Other times the journalist would try to make something up, and I knew immediately when they were trying to do it. You could always tell if these people (a) didn't know shit about you or (b) were trying to get you to say something off the wall so the extra little headline got them paid a bit more. The ones who were genuine were cool, though, but you'd run into those on maybe one out of ten occasions. I'd get irate with the bad ones sometimes, especially in Europe. They'd ask me a dumb question and I'd just say, "Eh, no" merely to piss them off. And then they'd get all irritated and ask, "Well, can you tell us *why* not?" To which I'd just say, "Then this interview is fuckin' over with, how's *that*?"

I remember one time in Paris this guy turned up in a motorcycle helmet and leathers to interview Dime and me for some fucking French metal magazine. He started getting all François with us, asking stupid questions like, "Well, why you don't have two more guitar players in your band?" What kind of a dumb question is that? We always wanted to go for the one guitar player, Van Halen–type of vibe, everyone knew that.

"Have you heard this one dude? Have you heard this mother-fucker right here?" I said, pointing at Dime. "That's all *we* need."

"Well…" he said.

"There's no 'well,' dude. This is just the way it is. You want an interview or don't you?"

"I am just asking the questions because blah blah blah…"

"You know what, you're fucking out of here, dude." And with that I took his helmet, threw it down the fucking stairs, and then I decided to throw his leather jacket, too—*while* he was still wearing it. There's a pivotal point right there at the back of the collar, and another lower down near the bottom of the back, so you can grab it there and with a swing backwards, then forwards, you're good to go!

That wasn't the only time this kind of thing happened. Occasionally I snapped when somebody asked me stupid questions. In the end, instead of banging heads with the press, I tried to run from the media attention, and when you've got a load of money, escape is that much easier. The press likes to build you up and then blow you down like a fucking tower. A similar thought occurred to me the other day when I heard that they were blowing up the Texas Stadium where the Dallas Cowboys played for years. There were some great memories within that place—some great games and the whole bit—but all these people turned up just to watch the place fall to the ground. I thought, "Haven't you got something better to do with your day than being there to watch that?" They had some chick over there with a Kleenex box, crying, and I just thought it was the dumbest thing I've ever seen in my life. The press likes to do the same thing with musicians, build them up and then tear them down. Even worse, many people like to read about it.

Thank fuck *TMZ* wasn't around back in those days, because I would have probably done myself in. I couldn't have coped with that level of privacy invasion. I sure as hell didn't get into all this to get my face on the cover of *People* magazine, and Philip certainly didn't either. If fame came our way, then let it come when we were up on stage. But with Vinnie and, to a lesser extent, Darrell, things were different: it's like they actually *wanted* all that attention.

The self-promotion and narcissism got so bad, especially by Vinnie. He would get our tour manager Guy Sykes to call from our bus into the strip club that we're sitting *outside* of, so that we'd get in for free, sit at a VIP table, and the whole bit. As we'd walk in it would be Vinnie and Val, our head of security, and then someone would announce in a melodramatic fashion, "Hey everyone, it's Vinnie Paaaaauuul from Pantera!"

Dime and I would be in the back, looking at Vinnie, and thinking, "Oh no, not again." Then we'd stare at each other and say, "Who the fuck *is* this dude anyway? Where does this shit come from? This guy wouldn't be anything if it wasn't for us," but Vinnie just had to bask in the spotlight.

The irony is that it didn't matter what these titty bars were like— and remember we hit every single one in every city we went to over a period of ten years. Some of them were so shitty that the girls had to put twenty-five cents in the jukebox themselves to play their favorite song before they got up onstage. Just to piss Vinnie off we used to say, "What the fuck have you got security rolling with you for anyway?" as if to question that he was important enough to even need security. As a band we were against that kind of crap. There were certain situations where we had to have it, in-store signings and shit like that, but we never had bodyguards just to look like rock stars. Vinnie, on the other hand, wanted stardom so badly he wanted to look like one, too.

THE ROCK STAR LIFESTYLE became extremely hard for all of us in the later era, particularly for me, partly because my kids were so young and I was torn between home life and life on the road, and also because the way I was living seemed a million miles away from the tough upbringing I had known. At the peak of our career in the mid-'90s we were selling tens of thousands of records every week and selling out amphitheaters wherever we went: at home and in Europe, South America, Japan, Australia, the whole world . . . We conquered them all and so we were all very wealthy dudes who were recognized wherever we went. We were always a fan's band, right from the very beginning when we relied on the Texas club crowd to literally put clothes on our back, and they did it just because they were totally into the music we were playing, which is something I've never forgotten. But when the public attention reached its peak toward the end of the '90s and more so still after Darrell's death, it felt like we were victims of our fan-friendly approach and it was definitely tough knowing how to respond.

Imagine being in a bar having a quiet drink and knowing *immediately* that the guy walking in the door recognizes you as Rex from Pantera. I could tell if that was the case from fifty fucking paces. A lot of times the person might have met you at a show somewhere or at an in-store, but what they forget is that I've seen thousands of faces over the years. Don't get me wrong, I don't mind friendly fans and a few photos and the whole bit, because God knows we wouldn't stop signing after shows until every single kid was happy. But it becomes an issue when people start *wanting* something more from you because of who you are. That kind of pressure just made me want to isolate myself further.

! # ⊕ *

I'M SOMEBODY WHO has dedicated his entire life to rock 'n' roll, and I *survived*. I came out the other end of my own dark avenue, shaken for sure, but having endured occupational hazards of this business like alcohol and drugs. Not only did I survive, but I also pride myself in having been a stand-up type of guy all the way down the line.

I've had a lot of help from upstairs, you know. That's the way I like to put it. I don't care what anyone else believes or doesn't believe. That's their deal, but for me, I believe in God although I don't subscribe to any particular organized religion.

I like to simplify it and say that I know the Ten Commandments—what to do and what not to—but I also believe that something higher and much greater than me has helped me get through the more traumatic side of a life in rock 'n' roll. I've always believed that you have to fight for what you want in life, and God knows I did, but you also have to have the good graces of something spiritually bigger than you to give you that little extra assistance. I didn't really realize all this until more recently, and occasionally I will get down on my knees and pray. Or I might just shut my eyes and take two minutes to take in the day; that achieves the same thing.

Despite how difficult life became, it's impossible to ignore the fact that playing music and my unbreakable desire to do so is what put me where I am. I have always viewed my life as a musical journey, and while there are good and bad aspects in everything I have been through to date, I never would have had any of it without the upbringing that I had. So if my story is going to start anywhere, then it would have to be in Texas.

CHAPTER 2

DADDY BILL

The town of Graham, Texas, isn't renowned for a whole lot of anything, maybe except that it's one of the only towns in all of Texas that still has a drive-in movie theater and nowadays they even have a Walmart. It was mainly an oil and cattle town since its inception, and although we lived in one of the smaller houses in our neighborhood, we definitely had one of the nicer properties I'm told, although obviously I don't remember.

CHERYL PONDER, sister

Mother, Daddy, and I moved to Graham in '57, and Rex was born in '64, and at that time Daddy was working for Texas Electric in the downtown office. Our house was in a really nice part of town because that was important to my mother. I remember asking her why her car sat broke in the driveway for so long and she said that she chose to have a nice place to live over anything else. She was trying to teach me about priorities.

————

When I was three years old we moved to De Leon. This little peanut-farming town with a population of 2,000 is located maybe seventy miles due south of Graham in very rural Texas. My dad—"Daddy Bill" as he was known—worked for Texas Electric and the move was a promotion for him, and he now was responsible for the electrical grids of three towns in Northern Texas. My mother never really worked and by this point my older sister Cheryl had gotten married and had moved out of the family home to live with her husband Buddy in the Dallas area, leaving me, Mom, and Dad in our house. It was a regular, three-bedroom place, not too big but big enough, with a huge yard that was home to countless dogs over my childhood years.

It was definitely rural Texas, you couldn't deny that. I remember walking to the end of the street and suddenly there were no more houses. Civilization stopped and was replaced by wild patches of watermelon as far as the eye could see.

One constant feature in the Brown household was music, and part of the varied soundtrack to my young life was my mother's vinyl repertoire, which included a whole bunch of swing bands, Tommy Dorsey mainly, and other acts like the Andrews Sisters and Louis Armstrong. My mother would pipe this stuff *every day* through this annoying intercom we had throughout the house, even to wake me up for school. That really began to piss me off. Looking back now, it was almost as if I was being *force-fed* music. Music always seemed to be played by *someone* in the house, either by my mother or my sister, who fortunately left me all her Elvis and Beatles 45s after she moved to the city, so I really didn't have a choice but to listen.

CHERYL PONDER

Music runs deep in our family. I really, truly believe that it's genetic. Our grandmother went to college in the early 1900s and got a music degree, purely by playing by ear. As I've grown to know second cousins more recently, it turns out that their son is very interested in music and wants to be in a band.

———

My Daddy Bill loved music, too, mainly big band stuff as well, and to accompany that pastime he was what you might call a social drinker. I mean, who wasn't in those days? I suppose it was because he'd grown up in the World War II–era where social drinking was an acceptable thing to do for middle class Americans. Basically it seemed like when they came back from the war everyone got fucking drunk and nobody really thought anything of it. Alcohol *was* a presence in our family tree though, and I later found out that while most of my relatives managed to function normally and hold down respectable jobs, quite a few were actually alcoholics. Apparently it's genetic.

CHERYL PONDER

Our father was a wonderful father. I wouldn't go as far as to say that he was a better father than he was a husband, but my parents were young when I grew up, and when Rex grew up, they weren't, and that gives me a slightly different perspective. Knowing our family like I do and Rex doesn't, alcoholism runs rampant in both sides of our family tree. Mother drank socially, and both her brothers were alcoholics in later years, and that trait goes all the way back as far as our great-great-grandfather, who was also an alcoholic.

———

My parents were also proud Presbyterians and our family attended church regularly throughout my childhood, but because De Leon was such a small place, the only church denomination that was available was Methodist, so we just went there every Sunday anyway. But while my parents were religious in that they believed in good morals and living correctly, they definitely didn't take it to the fire-and-brimstone level.From a young age—from the time I could walk and talk in fact—I was a ham. Anyone who was in a bad mood just needed to take one glance at my face and they'd have no choice but to laugh or at the very least smile. My sister tells me that whenever she used to visit for the weekend, when she pulled up in the driveway I'd always be standing there dressed up as something different: a cowboy, Superman, Batman, or frankly anything besides myself. I must have been born with a built-in need to perform.

One of our dogs was called Reddy Kilowatt—not exactly a normal dog name, I know, but he was named after the mascot used for electricity generation in the United States, and there's a picture of me with him somewhere where I'm dressed up as the Lone Ranger. And I did these things because I always wanted to be noticed. Fortunately, my dad's parents encouraged me to express myself. They lived just a half hour away in Ranger, Texas, and my grandparents, while very, very strict people, were also extremely influential on my early life and encouraged me to try anything I wanted to do. After all, I was the last of twenty-six grandchildren on both sides of the family, so it seemed that because they knew they'd probably never get another chance to be grandparents, I got special treatment.

Dad was diagnosed with cancer of the sinus cavity in 1971 and we had a maid to help my mom after Dad got sick, and she was called—brace yourself—"Nigger" Georgia. That's the name I always heard being called in the house. Sounds terrible, doesn't it? No wonder I've had problems with that word ever since. I grew to resent it because I didn't feel that it was proper. I didn't realize this as a kid though—it wasn't until much later in life that I came to know what that word truly meant, but that's just what my mother said—she made it sound like a term of endearment: "Nigger Georgia this, Nigger Georgia that." Nowadays I will never use the words "nigger" or "faggot," nor will I allow them to be used in my house. In my eyes, they are the foulest words imaginable.

I'm not trying to say that my mother was a racist—she definitely wasn't, but there were just very few black families out in the peanut farming areas at that time, and to talk like that was just how the South was back in the sixties and early seventies. Even at school you could see it: some of the water fountains were clearly marked, "Colored Only," which seems unbelievable in modern times, although I wouldn't be surprised if they are still there in some of the really back-ass places.

Because my dad was ill, it was easier for my mother to help him if I wasn't around all the time, so I was always being shuffled off to spend time with other people, especially my maternal grandmother, who lived in downtown Ft. Worth. Well, she was quite a woman, let me tell you. Back in the day, she and her brother Jack lived in Thurber, Texas—right on the county line—one of the only places you could get liquor back in the '30s and '40s post-prohibition days. That was where all the juke joints were back in the day, in hard-living towns like Strawn, Mingus, and Thurber. My grandmother used to play the piano down at the front in the silent movies that were shown in these tough little towns in the Texas countryside.

She used to tell me stories about when, back in those days after prohibition, she and her brother Jack—who played standup bass—had a band. When they were up on stage performing, everybody in the audience got so drunk that, when they didn't like a song, they'd just throw a fucking beer bottle at the musicians in protest. So the only way to stop being hit on the head by a bunch of beer bottles was to hang chicken wire around the stage area, like some kind of crude barricade. I'm sure some missiles still got through though. These places were rough, and you can probably still find dives like this in some outlying parts of the state.

She lived in this huge Victorian home with another elderly lady. I can still remember the place like I was there last week. Isn't it weird how places stick in your head from when you're a kid, but you can't remember seemingly more important things for shit? The place she lived in was divided into a bunch of apartments, and her place was on the second floor.

My grandmother was an amazing person in many ways, but her complete immersion in music influenced the young me most—she was certainly one of the primary reasons that I became interested in playing it. She was so delicate and one of those people who had a natural talent for everything musical. As a five-year-old I used to sit on her knee while she played piano, absorbing every sight and sound in complete fascination. As if to confirm that I might have been a musical instrument aficionado while still in the womb, I even remember the piano itself. It was one of those stand-up types—don't ask me the *exact* model. She would just sit there and casually play along to Joplin and Charles Mingus—cats like that—as if it was the easiest thing in the world, and that added more to the amazing mixture of music styles that I was being exposed to as a child.

! # ⊕ *

AT THIS TIME, something my young head didn't fully grasp was just how sick my dad actually was. You don't analyze it when you're young, I don't think. In fact I suspect all of us—Dad included—were in denial about just how bad things were, and I think all of us felt that if we didn't talk about it, it somehow wasn't there. But it was there. And because Dad was worried that he'd lose his job if his employers found out how sick he was, and that he might not be able to fulfill his daily duties, his ill health was never really discussed, and especially not outside the four walls of the Brown household.

So as a young kid, I'd happily go off to school while mom would drive him to the city for treatment, and I guess I just thought that he was in the hospital getting better when actually he was dying, his body systematically eaten up by cancer. Back in the '70s there wasn't the technology available to catch cancer early enough to stop it spreading like wildfire—they just dealt with it when they found it, often too late. And when they *did* find it, all they had at their disposal was chemo or radiation, so Dad had to stay in the hospital in the city, getting dosed with one or the other. I remember going to visit him and because of how sick it made him feel, the only food he could taste and enjoy was fried catfish washed down with Budweiser, so we would always sneak some in there for him. Sounds like a weird combination I know, but it was all he seemed to want.

CHERYL PONDER

Daddy was diagnosed in April of 1971 and had extensive and immediate radiation for six weeks, which didn't seem to slow it down much. Because it was cancer of the nasal pharynx, it seemed to be hard to contain. Then in the summer of the same year he had another biopsy and it was still spreading.

———

Although I was young and he was sick for most of the time I knew him, my dad and I did have a close bond. When you consider that my sister is seventeen years my senior, it's easy to see why, too. Because Cheryl and I had basically grown up in two separate generations of our parents' lives, and he just adored me, even though I suspect I was one of those mistakes after they went to the country club and got drunk one night.

I have dim memories of us sitting on the couch in the afternoons watching golf together. He loved having me for company even though I clearly knew very little about golf. Something about the game must have permeated my psyche though and the Colonial tournament sticks out in my mind particularly—probably because it was played locally in Ft. Worth, and he stressed that very fact to me at the time. I know that he would have been really proud to know that his son would get invited to play in it in later life.

Even while he was very sick he would still drink Budweiser like it was going out of fucking style. So at the age of five I probably tasted my first beer, and as shocking as that might sound, that's just how my dad was. He'd just slide me a sip of his beer when my mom wasn't watching and I'd drink it. I can't imagine that I liked it but at least I was giving my body plenty of year's head start to develop a taste for it. For the record, I couldn't imagine feeding my five-year-old a fucking beer nowadays, but back in the day that's just how things were.

CHERYL PONDER

Mother had no idea how to become a widow or a single parent at the age of forty-seven, so along the way she'd made a lot of psychological mistakes, which she couldn't redo. She knew it but she couldn't go back and redo. I would call every other day to see how Daddy was, and if mother saw one little glimmer of what she thought was "Oh, he's going to get better" then we all thought he was going to get well, and Rex got caught in the middle of all that. Back in the '70s, I'm not sure if many people knew much about psychology, or at least how to tell a young child that his dad is dying.

Predictably—due to my dad's poor health—most of the parenting and disciplining was left to my mother, although she had a few health issues of her own. She'd had polio as a child and while there were no lingering effects that could be clearly identified, when Dad got really sick she didn't cope well at all and it triggered a central nervous reaction that impaired the use of her limbs. What that meant was that in order to take care of Dad while her mobility decreased, I got farmed out to stay with other people more and more, sometimes to people that I hardly knew.

Apart from grandparents' houses on both sides of the family, one of my other favorite places to go was my uncle's beach house place at Surfside, south of Galveston, because when I was there, I was basically there on my own, free to roam the sand dunes that stretched out for four hundred yards and free to get in the ocean and try to learn to surf, mostly unsuccessfully, I might add.

Strangely, even at this young age, I seemed to like fending for myself, scrapping to survive, and this was a trait I'd carry throughout my life. Whether it was because I had no choice or because I was a naturally independent type, who knows? Not only was it a way of protecting myself, but it was also indicative of a kind of single-minded drive that I would always possess. Yes, I was a small, skinny kid, but I always punched above my weight in every sense.

CHERYL PONDER

Rex was always full of it. He had a great little personality but he did pretty much exactly whatever he wanted, wherever he was. He thought he was independent from a very young age.

———

My dad passed away in January of 1972, almost exactly a year after his own father had passed, and I get the impression from what I've been told that it was a long and painful death. He was only forty-seven-years old. Young by anybody's standards.

I was oblivious.

This is where it gets sticky for me. I'm not the kind to open up too much emotionally, and my dad's passing is something I have never discussed with anyone, not even my mother or sister. I must have completely shut it out immediately because at that age I had no hope of coming to terms with what death actually meant, although I'm surprised about how much I actually remember about the events themselves.

On the day he died I was playing outside in the yard at the doctor's house, the biggest mansion in town, as if it was any other day, and my mother came out to tell me that Daddy had passed. Although I was still very young, I can still vividly remember that the first thing my mother said was, "I don't know what I'm going to do."

Of course I didn't have an answer. I was a kid. I just kept playing…

CHAPTER 3

ON DOWN THE LINE

With no father, and a mother who was struggling to cope both physically and emotionally, the road ahead could have been a grim proposition. I missed having my dad around of course, but because I had never experienced some of the things that kids experience with their fathers—learning to nail a curveball or how to catch a football—I couldn't really say that I felt I missed out on that kind of fatherly input, because you can't miss what you never had. All I do remember is that it seemed that people in the neighborhood took pity on me in an "Oh, poor kid. He lost his dad early" type of bullshit way, but I just carried on doing what kids do, playing in the street, riding around town on my bike, and the whole bit. Life's got to go on...

CHERYL PONDER

Mother had the beginnings of a condition that's related to muscular dystrophy, triggered—in many cases—by trauma. She'd had polio as a child but had never had any lingering effects of that, but after Daddy died she started falling for no reason. At that time she could pick herself up and do whatever she needed to do but as time went on, her condition got worse and she ended up having to go into a wheelchair.

————

After two and a half more years in De Leon, mother made the decision to move us to Arlington in June of 1974. It made sense of course. We were only ever in De Leon because of Dad's job, so with him gone, there was no reason to stay because we had no other attachment to the place whatsoever. Apparently Mom briefly considered moving back to Graham, but it would have been hard without Dad and—perhaps more significantly—the city seemed a better move so that we could all be closer to my sister Cheryl and her husband Buddy.

Sometime after we left, my young life radically changed. While listening to music in my bedroom one night, I remember hearing the most fucking amazing sound emerging from my radio, and don't forget, it was still only AM radio in those days. The name of the song was "Tush" and the band was ZZ Top, and when I heard this song, it immediately altered my outlook on everything. I held onto that feeling for dear life. Even as a young boy, I knew exactly what the blues was. I heard it being played all the time and in lots of different forms. I'd heard the Rolling Stones, who definitely had blues roots, and I'd also been exposed to the Beatles, who, while still having vague hints of blues hidden in the background, seemed to my ears much more like innovators within pop culture. But this was in a completely different and new style. ZZ Top was a new type of boogie, a new stomp, and I *really* dug it.

"Dallas, Texas, Hollywooooo–ood…" You know how it goes and that to me was fucking telling. My first thought was, "Screw this; I want an electric guitar now. This is what I've got to do. Got to do." Until this point, I hadn't been the kind of kid that had posters of bands on my wall—I was much more into sports and shit like that—but that was all going to change. I was probably only eight years old at the time.

So, after we moved to the city and when I showed up for my first day at my new school, I was faced with total culture shock. Hell, I was used to having eight kids in my class—maybe ten—and now all of a sudden I'm in a 5th grade classroom with fifty kids, split over three partitions. It took a while to adjust, and as a result of feeling lost in the crowd, I started acting like the class clown to get attention while hopefully making some new friends.

CHERYL PONDER

The main reason for mother and Rex moving into the city was to be near my husband and I. I wanted to help mother with Rex, and the opportunities were better for Rex in Arlington.

———

Even at this age I would take anyone on. I was a scrappy little dude for sure. I had no fear whatsoever and because I didn't, the bigger kids soon became my friends, but usually only after I'd tried to smash their skull in a fight. I had no problem tackling someone who was a foot taller than me, and lots of kids were in those days. I used to whoop some ass back then, as that was only way I could guarantee respect, and if things went wrong, I always knew I could run faster than them anyway.

I guess you could compare my approach to what it would be like going into prison for the first time, where you hit the biggest guy you can get your fucking hands on in order to get immediate respect. All the other inmates would say, "Fuck, this dude must be badass," and would leave you alone. That's how I had to live my life. Remember, I had no father, my mother would never re-marry, and while my sister's husband Buddy would do his level best to fill the paternal role, I pretty much had to raise myself.

My mom *did* do her best, though, and she definitely wanted to instill good morals in me. She also wanted to get me into something that kept me occupied, so the local church—the First Presbyterian denomination to be precise—fitted both bills because it had a really good youth squad. *And* there were a lot of hot chicks there. I don't know whether I went more for strictly religious reasons or for the interaction with chicks, but I'm sure you can figure that out.

Either way, I sang in the church choir and had a lot of other activities going on that were connected to the church. Mom wanted to keep me really busy with singing trips—camps where you'd go away for a week on a bus to sing in different cities, that kind of thing. We'd go to the Little Rocks, the Shreveports, all over the place really, staying with other families from other parishes. Then we'd do our little bit during their Sunday service, and usually I was singing lead in *something*, I was that good.

The choir director's name was Michael Kemp, and when I look back on it, he really helped bring out my talent by making me feel comfortable singing in front of an audience and the whole bit. He wasn't a father figure as such, but he was definitely a mentor and he saw the talent and probably already knew that I was going to be some kind of a musician.

This church was cliquey though. Not only was the size of its congregation large, it was also organized religion to the extreme—while I probably didn't see the writing on the wall at the time, in terms of what organized religion actually was, I was aware that it seemed to be all about who's got the most money, who's got the best shoes or the biggest house, and all that. Maybe when you're going through your formative years you don't really pay too much attention to the wider issues of a subject like organized religion; other things seem much more important. There are enough school studies that you're trying to deal with, so a class subject such as religious study was just one more on a long list I had to take.

CHERYL PONDER

The church had a very active youth group. In 1975, the church hired a new music director called Michael Kemp, and he and his wife had just gotten their degrees in music and moved to Arlington. He was just so talented and he put together a church choir with the kids, and our daughter Charlotte and Rex joined and immediately. Michael took to Rex because he could see the talent that he had. The kids went on all kinds of trips, and Mike became increasingly proud of Rex, gave him more and more responsibility.

———

While you could hardly say that I was an academic genius in class, I did take my studies seriously but always with this underlying sense that the subjects weren't going to be too relevant to my future career, almost as if I knew my destiny. Fortunately I didn't have to try too hard and was a solid B-student—initially at least—because I always had this insatiable appetite for knowledge. I always liked to read books: history, geography, you name it, I read them. I still do.

Around the same time I got into junior high band, which was an important move in the right direction for my musical aspirations but a backward step for my academics. Of course I wanted to be on the drum line because that's where all the good stuff was—the part of the band that was most fun—but they needed me somewhere else.

So they pretended that they needed some of the brighter kids in there or certainly ones that were more qualified than I was, which didn't make sense because I played in the beginner band, the middle band, and the superior band, and was All City and All State in music, and that would continue until I was in tenth grade in high school. The "somewhere else" they referred to would soon be clear.

What they didn't have were any tuba players. So they thought, "Shit, this kid weighs ninety pounds, let's go ahead and strap this fuckin' sixty-pound tuba on him and make him ride the bus with it and walk all the way up a hill with this thing to practice." Naturally, I thought this was the dumbest thing ever—but it turned out to be the right choice because it was excellent musical training and I got good at it in a hurry.

CHERYL PONDER

Rex getting into the little school band as a tuba player was the most significant moment musically for him, other than the fact that we had all always enjoyed *listening* to music. But him actually learning to *play* an instrument was a big step forward.

———

Like most kids my age, I played baseball, excelling at pitcher and shortstop. I played soccer until I got tired of running after a ball, and I played football, despite being too small to initially get on the football team. What I did have in my favor was my dad's legs. He held the record for the hundred-meter dash in the state of Texas for seventeen years, and I could certainly cover the ground and catch the ball. Eventually somebody pulled some strings somewhere and got me on the team, but the coach—who was a total dick—just made me be a towel boy or a water boy. That was a shitty role, and all the bigger kids would tease me by sticking my head down the toilet and flushing it, known as a "swirlie." Who needs a head/mouthful of shit?

Thankfully I had this one good friend then who I'll call Jack and at times I needed him so God bless him. He was this huge black dude—biggest guy on the team by far—and for reasons I never really understood, he took me under his wing like a guardian angel. I think he had missed about five grades of school, but whenever I had any troubles during my junior high and high school days, Jack seemed to appear out of nowhere. I lost touch with him in high school when he got into some heavy-duty drug dealings and ended up in jail, so who knows where he is now. Actually, he may be one of those characters who'll be in jail his whole life, but I'll never forget him for how he always took my side.

CHERYL PONDER

Rex pitched for a little league team which my husband Buddy helped coach, and he also played football for the Lancers football team that might have won a championship of some kind at one point.

While sports were still holding my interest somewhat, I had started to listen to a lot of music. Pop culture was about to undergo radical change, and I could now pick up FM rock radio 'cause we lived in the Dallas Metroplex area where there was a bigger tower. I couldn't have chosen a better moment to start exploring the radio dial.

Better still, because FM was stereo, the whole dynamics of songs just got bigger and more in your face. Bread were a big band at this time and got a lot of airplay, and then because of them I got into bands like America and James Taylor. After immersing myself into this acoustic style of music, I quickly worked out how to play most of the chords. Another turning point for me was when my cousins in Midland, Texas, played me Stevie Wonder's *Songs in the Key of Life*, not the kind of stuff you'd imagine I would like, but it really left its mark from a songwriting and arranging point of view. I actually thought that record, in a weird way, was better than a lot of the Beatles stuff that my sister had introduced me to.

While my mom was supportive of me learning music—she bought me all the books and scribes to help me read music—she was also insistent that I made something of my life. Problem was, her idea of "making something" was getting a job. She had this ingrained attitude that if you didn't finish out high school, you were doomed to spending your life as a ditch digger.

CHERYL PONDER

Mother and I wanted Rex to get an education. And I say "Mother and I" because I was very much part of watching him grow up, run away a couple of times, and just not do the things that any parent would want their children to do. Rex was so smart—so smart—but he just didn't apply himself, and both mother and I were frustrated. My daughter Charlotte was only fifteen months younger than Rex and she was an excellent student, so I think there was a little jealousy there between the two of them because they were so close in age. We just wanted him to at least get his high school diploma and then he could go on and do what his music was going to do. Granted, the chance he took was one in a million and he succeeded but as a parent, it's not what you would choose for your child because you have nothing to fall back on.

All I knew was that I had something in me that was going to drive me to do something with music. Something was taking me down this path, and I had no choice but to follow it and learn all I could along the way. My first guitar had these terrible strings that had never been changed. It sucked. I had calluses all over my hands but I never thought to get any new strings until someone told me that I should.

Unperturbed by substandard gear, I started taking lessons at the YMCA because it was cheap—ten dollars a month or something. I'd go in there and play whatever the teacher had for the day. He gave me a John Denver book of songs to take home, and when everyone came to our house for the holidays, I'd play all these songs and sing them, too, which is kind of embarrassing to think about now.

As a resource, the YMCA was effective because they had all the books and the chords readily available, but it seemed like with the guitar you had to change chords with every beat or measure. So I decided to pick up something entirely new: the *bass* guitar, even though I could already play piano, drums, and guitar pretty well, and my ability to read music was already off the map.

CHAPTER 4

REX, DRUGS, AND ROCK 'N' ROLL

By the time ninth grade rolled around, my first class of the day was jazz band—that was cool—and the second class was English. Except I didn't show up for English—I showed up at the park near my house instead. They didn't do shit about truancy in those days so I'd just take off, burn one, and throw a fucking Frisbee around.

Now, a Frisbee was a key part of my teenage apparatus, and here's why: You learn how to roll a joint on the Frisbee, get all the seeds out of it, and get rid of all the crap. Some Frisbees had a little recess where you could hide something inside, so you'd light the joint, put it in the Frisbee, and throw it to your buddy. He'd then smoke the joint and throw it back, and all of this is happening while everyone else was taking English class. This was *my* education.

If I decided to go back for the third class of the day it was algebra, a class I shared with Vinnie Paul Abbott. I'd known of him because we'd both been in All City bands and stuff like that—he in the drum line—so I'd been aware of vaguely who he was, not least because it seemed he'd had a full beard and moustache since he was about eleven years old. He was one hairy dude. He also had these huge, double canine teeth, and I'd go out to lunch with him from time to time, but at that point I thought of him as an acquaintance rather than a good friend. Though I guess we were friends in some ways—music taste being the main common bond—in other ways we weren't.

There was, however, a significant advantage to this almost-friendship. Vinnie's dad Jerry had the only proper recording studio in town that I knew of and was its sound engineer, He also wrote a bunch of country songs that he was always trying to sell. I think he'd done some songs for ABC Records back in the day. Through him and Vinnie, I got to meet his brother Darrell, who at that point couldn't play the guitar to save his life. Darrell was a couple of years younger and he was just a scrawny little skateboard punk in those days.

By now I was listening to pretty much anything that was current, absorbing it all. Vinnie sat in front of me in algebra class and we soon got into talking about bands and players, usually while the teacher was talking, too. His big thing in those days was Neil Peart, Rush's drummer and lyricist, and if you didn't like what Vinnie liked, it was his way or the highway. He'd say bullshit stuff to me like, "Dude, Neil Peart ... he blows John Bonham away." I still followed ZZ Top, of course, and then all of a sudden here comes bands like Bad Company, and when I got into them, my naturally inquisitive nature brought me *back* to understand Black Sabbath and Zeppelin, and where that all came from because that stuff was more progressive. To me, the first Zeppelin record sounded more like Jeff Beck's *Truth* album, and Jeff was always one of my favorite guitar players.

So, being a huge Zeppelin fan by then already I'd say, "Are you out of your fuckin' mind?" And then the teacher would interrupt our vital debate and bust our asses for talking in class.

"Brown, Abbott! Pay attention!"

Incidentally, the reason I have no ass at all nowadays is because I was paddled every fucking day. Remember when they'd drill holes in the back of the paddle to make it sting like shit? Well, I got a lot of that treatment. But after a while you just *have* to just start laughing, which of course they hated, so they'd say, "Do you want two more?" "Go ahead, I have no ass anyway, and you're probably gonna break my pelvis so it doesn't really matter ..." I'd reply, so my ass was never the same after that.

Soon, Led Zeppelin's *Physical Graffiti* record led me down a new and chemical path. I had this friend who used to get balls of opium, and we'd sit with a hot knife over a stove with hash and opium listening to that record nonstop while catching this killer buzz. This would be my first real experience with drugs, and when I did it I took a whole lot of them. There were no half measures. Then I took acid and that was just wild, and I knew I'd found a whole new me. We did blue-dot or paper and I got hallucinations that I couldn't get from smoking pot, and they would last for eight to twelve fucking hours. Better still, all the music we were listening to seemed to be *enhanced* by the drugs, songs like Floyd's "Comfortably Numb," already a trippy song, but while high on drugs it took me to another planet. This stuff and my sister's Beatles albums were the perfect sound-tracks to my acid trips.

The evolution of rock music interested me almost as much as listening to it or playing an instrument. It might sound strange but it was almost as if I knew that I was going to be part of the rock scene one day, so it made sense for me to want to understand how and why I would arrive at that final destination.

To me it all started with the Delta blues, with someone like Robert Johnson. From there you can trace it through to Howlin' Wolf, Chicago blues, and I know that step skips a lot of time and a lot of great blues players who were out there, but that's the general progression as I heard it. So you could say that the origin of rock and roll comes from the Mississippi Delta all the way through Chuck

Berry to English bands like the Beatles, the Stones, and Zeppelin to where we are now. But it began in America, in the South.

I say all this for good reason apart from offering my view of the development of rock music. It always irritated me in later years when people referred to Pantera's sound as being "southern," as if that was something unusual. And musically speaking, the only thing "southern" about us was the fact that we happened to be from Dallas. As I've illustrated, *all* rock music originated from the southern states, so I always felt that Pantera's sound was misidentified. You couldn't label us or call us anything in my opinion; we just took our place in the line of rock music evolution.

In later life I learned to appreciate why being from the South affected our behavior. People are actually nicer and open doors for you down there, and I think a lot of that's because of how we are raised. I always carried that southern pride with me into every situation, and the misconception that the South is just a bunch of rednecks shooting guns is just plain wrong.

As my musical knowledge and appreciation diversified, so did my dress style—or more accurately, my *anti*-style. I always wore camping gear or the kind of attire you wear when you're climbing up a fucking mountain, which I often did on those Church outings. Jeans, hiking boots, flannel shirts, headband … that was what I liked to wear. Kind of that whole grunge look, but long before the grunge movement even existed.

I was singing (before my balls dropped, that is) and playing bass by this time in my first real band called Neck and the Brewheads, and we played around town covering stuff like the Stones, Zeppelin, a little bit of Rush—whatever was on FM radio at the time. Our drummer's brother used to play in the band Cactus, so that was part of our repertoire, too, because the kids could really relate to it.

We were playing for all the hippies. There was still that hippie hangover from the '60s, people hanging out and smoking grass, and that was definitely the crowd who gravitated to our shows. The '70s was a strange, transitional decade, and a lot of people were into that disco shit, so it was initially hard to get people into what we were playing. That was the year before I really got into heavy metal in a hardcore way—Iron Maiden, Judas Priest, and Motörhead—and we just played backyards and keg parties.

Here in Texas, someone would get permission to use an open field on somebody's land and they'd have a bunch of people over and fifteen kegs of beer. We were the most popular party band in town at that time; sometimes we'd get paid cash and other times the deal would simply be "give us all the beer we can drink and a hit of acid and we're good." Either option was just fine with me.

The Abbott brothers were two of the only kids in town with a proper PA system, because their dad had bought them one. Our singer also had a PA, but he would never show up to practice, so Vinnie and Darrell would let me borrow their board or mics or whatever, as long as I brought it back to the house the next day. They were always cool about letting me borrow the PA when they weren't using it. Their mother Carolyn would say, "Yeah, Rex, you can take it now. They're gone somewhere, doing something." So I had access to free gear whenever I needed it.

They had started their own band with Terry Glaze, Donnie Hart, and Tommy Bradford, and called it Pantera. The name doesn't have any deep significance. It was the name of a really fast car and also Spanish for "panther," that's all there is to it. It's just a cool name that hopefully people could identify with. They were actually pretty good but were mostly just playing in a garage. But when they did play shows, their crowd was completely different from my band. They played for all the yuppies. While Neck and the Brewheads were playing Zeppelin, Stones, and Nugent, Pantera were playing Loverboy— that was the difference at this point. Two *totally* different worlds.

By the time I'd reached the eleventh grade, my musical ability was of such a sufficiently high standard that I was being recruited by North Texas State University, one of the best musical schools in the entire country. They had probably the best lab band there ever was. Lab—short for "laboratory"—is a type of experimental jazz where you interpret Charlie Parker or any of that kind of stuff. Some great musicians have come out of that school, and they actually offered me a scholarship to attend.

But this was still the Frisbee days for me. I wanted no part of the academic world. I felt like I was born to play rock 'n' roll, not to learn material for another fucking jazz competition, so as strange as it might sound to have turned down a prestigious college, it was indicative of the kind of single-minded dedication to the vision I had for my true path in life: to live the life of a rock 'n' roller.

CHERYL PONDER

I remember mother telling me that Rex was in this garage band called Neck and the Brewheads, and from what I remember he'd go there to practice, stay gone until all hours of the night, so at first it was very hard for mother to deal with because she was at home on her own and by one o'clock in the morning he often wasn't home on school nights. Michael Kemp from the church used to come over to talk to Rex to try and show him that this was not the way to be a good kid. He probably felt that Michael turned on him when he sided with mother, but we all just wanted the best for Rex's future. Mike said, "Rex, you are such a good musician. Let me get you a scholarship. I can get you a scholarship to any college in the country with your talent," but Rex had no interest in that at all.

While I was doing my thing with Neck and the Brewheads and scrounging around every way I could to survive, the Abbott brothers were doing their own thing and getting a bit of a reputation in town. Little Dime was still only just learning the guitar, he could hardly even play fucking barre chords, but he steadily progressed until one summer in the early '80s, somebody gave him Ozzy Osbourne's *Blizzard of Ozz* and *Diary of a Madman*.

Dime then sequestered himself in his fucking bedroom for that entire summer, and when he came out he was a fucking virtuoso. It was that simple. His dad—who was left handed—had been helping him out, too, and not only could he play every note and chord that Randy Rhoads or Eddie Van Halen played, Dime could already put his own variations, his personality, on everything he played. It was this ability to improvise that made his guitar playing so plain fucking dangerous, even as a teenager. So whenever they had a show, I'd usually go along and hang out, and sometimes they'd get me to run the board and the whole bit.

TERRY GLAZE (original lead singer for the first three Pantera records)

All of a sudden Darrell could play "Eruption" by Van Halen. It was just flowing out of him, completely naturally, and around that time they were putting on some guitar shows in Dallas. So this little, skinny kid with a giant afro goes to the first one, demolishes everybody, and wins a Dean guitar. We were all there and he outdueled everyone; and then at the next competition, the winner won a Charvel strat and maybe a Randall halfstack, and Darrell won that one, too, and it was not even close. After that he was not allowed to be in any more competitions—so he became a judge. He also had one of the first Floyd Rose tremolos in Dallas if I remember correctly. We had only seen them in magazines or pictures of Van Halen, and we never really knew what it was. He found a guy in town that could fit one to his guitar so he took his Dean over there, the sunburst one, and put a Floyd Rose on there.

That was the year 1982 that everyone else graduated but because I skipped school, I didn't make that graduation class. (I'd been too busy rolling joints and playing Frisbee, remember.) Instead I got a G.E.D., and under the rules it stated that I either had to be in school full-time or have a part-time job, or else the benefits my mother received because of my dad's war veteran status would be cut in half.

Despite that, I jumped to junior college after lying about my age on the application form. Obviously they were always going to find out my real age and when they did, almost six weeks later, they kicked me out, saying, "Kid, you're just too young," even though I had the G.E.D., but I was always the youngest in every class because of when my birthday fell. Now what? I had to find some kind of employment, if for no other reason than to ease my mother's anxiety for my future.

CHERYL PONDER

I'm not sure how much sway a G.E.D. would have nowadays but back in the '70s it would probably get you into college after a couple of years sitting it out, but it was hard fought to get Rex to even understand that. Mother and Rex didn't always see eye to eye, and in retrospect they both probably needed some kind of psychological help but neither one of them got it.

———

So, to supplement my gig income—which at that time came mostly in liquid form—I had all kinds of jobs, the first of which taught me how to adapt to opportunities that might present themselves in order to make money. I worked out of a kiosk in the middle of a parking lot where I was supposed to be working for Fotomat, but that wasn't all I was doing.

You see, in those days I could buy these black beauties—speed—for sixty-five bucks and there would be maybe two thousand pills that I could sell for a buck each. So if somebody wanted to stop by and pick up a hundred, it was no problem because all I had to do was stick them in this little Fotomat roll-bag, void the ticket, and that was that. I used to sell acid out of this place, too, and if people wanted to come and get bulk, no problem, I'd sell them bulk. I made a fucking fortune as a little seventeen-year-old drug dealer. I'd leave for an hour to sleep or get high, come back, and there'd be guys beating on the doors and the windows, and all the while I was stoned out of my head. I worked at all these different Fotomat kiosks across county lines, and in most cases it was all about selling drugs, except when I was bored and I'd go through people's pictures and shit—you wouldn't believe some of the stuff I saw.

I had a great stroke of luck when I found some pictures of Randy Rhoads taken in 1980—young as you could imagine—so I called Darrell at 261-2260 (his home number; I'll never forget it) and said, "Dude, I've got this print you're not going to fucking believe." I pestered the fuck out of him until he took it off me—kind of a payback for loaning me their gear all those times—and I even fixed Terry Glaze and Vinnie up with jobs at Fotomat, too.

TERRY GLAZE

Working for Fotomat was a great job because when I worked there very few people would come by each day. I liked it because I was attending college so I could just sit in there, study, and get paid to do it.

In addition to selling all this kind of shit out of the kiosk, I'm also routinely swindling money off Fotomat by voiding tickets and pocketing the cash. I was a fucking hoodlum and in my mind it was all about survival. It's no surprise that I had some crazy-ass customers coming to these kiosks, but they had to be low-key or I wouldn't sell to them anymore. If I found out they were on the street talking they were fucked, *and* I'd charge them double.

When that ended, my mom got me a job placement at Texas Electric where my dad used to work. They had me doing the mail runs in a truck around the Ft. Worth area, after which I'd go home, sleep for two or three hours, and then we'd play the clubs until three in the morning. This went on for six months or so until I finally said, "I can't do this shit anymore" and tried to find something else.

CHAPTER 5

12 O'CLOCK HIGH

Darrell Abbott's on the phone, he wants to talk to you," my mom shouted from the garage door one night after I'd just gotten back from playing with my band Neck and the Brewheads.

"What does he want?" I asked her.

"I don't know. He just wants to talk to you," she told me.

It was eleven o'clock and my bass was still in the backseat of my car. I picked up the phone, and he asked me if I wanted to come to the studio and play some bass on some stuff. I was already baked—had already smoked about three joints and had drunk a quart or two of beer—but I got straight back in my car and went to the studio.

My mom probably shouted after me, "It's eleven-thirty at night, you should be in bed!" She could never get me to stay home at night. But, of course, I was already gone, so I wouldn't have heard her anyway.

When I got there they wanted me to play on three songs that would ultimately end up on the *Metal Magic* album and they were actively trying to get rid of their original bass player, a guy called Tommy Bradford, because he'd said he wanted to go in a different musical direction. So I just played naturally, did what I did, and we recorded these songs. I think that some of those originals actually ended up on the first record.

In my mind, Pantera made sense as a long-term deal because as good as we were, Neck and the Brewheads was really just a party band and all the boys were fixing to go to college anyway. But with the brothers I knew they were serious. We all had the same goal in mind and wanted to be the best that we could.

TERRY GLAZE

Vinnie and I had known each other from high school, and Vinnie was by the far the best drummer in the area. Me and my buddy Tommy Bradford, who played bass, wanted to put together a band and we desperately wanted Vinnie in it, but he said, "If you want me, you need to take my little brother Darrell also." He couldn't play too well at that time, but pretty soon he'd turn into a monster. We knew who Rex was, of course, because being such a small place, we'd heard that he played around town with his band. So when Tommy wanted to leave the band to do his own thing, we asked Rex to come down and do some overdubs on some tracks that would end up on the first record. Before Rex joined, we were basically a five-piece because we had a guy called Donnie Hart singing.

———

It was clear from the first session that I was their guy, or at least to me it was. They asked me to join properly on June 7, 1982. I was seventeen years old. I remember the day so well. They felt they had to lay down some basic ground rules: one, I had to quit smoking and two, I couldn't drink, so when I walked into my first rehearsal as a band member, I had a cigarette hanging out of my mouth and a six pack of Löwenbräu under my arm. That is the fucking truth and that's how it all began.

Understand that the guys were really straight-edged in the early days, almost clueless when it came to drugs and alcohol. They didn't drink, certainly never touched drugs, and hadn't really opened their minds to music or the rocker lifestyle like I already had. All they wanted to do was play Def Leppard, which I was into as well. (*High 'n' Dry* was just out, I think.) Because from seventh to eleventh grade I'd had all this musical experience and the best theoretical grounding possible for a young kid, I always had a perfect pitch. I could pretty much listen to a record—and when I say record I mean a track—and pick out exactly what needed to be played, whereas with other cats it could take them a long time to get something down.

TERRY GLAZE

I wanted to write songs and if I was going to do that, I was going to want to sing them, too. So Donnie Hart left and I became the singer in what was now the four-piece Pantera. Rex sang backing vocals, Vinnie sang a lot, too, but Darrell just stood there and your jaw dropped. Regardless of whether we were playing little country towns or city shows, Darrell was the guy that kept the people in the room. Even at that time I knew that I was in the company of someone truly incredible, and the cool thing about him was that he never tried to make you feel that he was so much better than you. He was just like a big kid.

So, you could say that I brought much more experience to the table than they did in terms of musical ability, and certainly some much-needed street smarts. There was payback though: they wanted me to play in fucking spandex, and at first I just totally refused to get into that slippery shit. I wanted to stick to my own style because I liked to think image didn't matter. Then here comes all these bands that really relied on image, and I had to confess that when the first Mötley Crüe record came out I realized that all the leather actually looked really cool. So what the fuck, there I was soon enough borrowing my first pair of spandex from Dime. I didn't like it but it was what we had to do to get in the clubs and establish any kind of attraction from the crowd.

RITA HANEY (girlfriend of Darrell Abbott)

I knew Darrell before I knew Rex but I got to know Rex best around high school time, that's when he came into the picture and he was wiry, feisty, and pretty rebellious. Darrell used to tell me all the time how he'd run into Rex in different places and Rex would say, "I'm going to play bass for you," but at the time he had a broken arm from a skateboarding accident. Darrell just blew him off but when they did audition him, he showed up doing the exact things Darrell told him not to do!

Because we were young and hired the cheapest booking agents possible, we took any kind of gig we could get our hands on: proms, bar mitzvahs, whatever was out there. Initially we only played around Dallas but soon we'd be travelling up to six hours away to parts of Oklahoma and Louisiana to do more shows and because we weren't old enough to get into clubs, Jerry Abbott (AKA "the old man") would need to come out and (a) get us in and (b) try—in vain—to keep us on the straight and narrow.

Jerry would make Dime and me share a room, and that was a mistake because this is when I finally got Dime to check out drinking. We had this roadie who was of age and would buy us bottles of Jack, so we'd just shut the lights off and climb out the window to drink while the old man was asleep in the room next door. Now that Dime had started drinking, he steadily took it to a higher and higher level—good Lord did he ever.

Some of these trips would be weekend gigs and others would be week-long residencies, but no matter what the deal was, we played three sets a night with the first and third sets being covers and the middle one being original stuff. Because we were from the South, we inevitably gravitated toward playing blues riffs. Then we moved on to playing cover tunes of guys *trying* to play blues riffs. Some of the songs we were doing were typical Top-40 repertoire, too: the heaviest Dokken song you could find on their record, for example, just to draw the crowd, but we tried to limit that and focus more on classic rock and blues stuff or whatever was hot off the radio.

TERRY GLAZE

In these days most bands in the area were just like we were, except in almost every other case, those bands attracted an audience of mostly girls whereas we attracted young guys. Now, that's not because we weren't particularly good-looking, it was definitely because Darrell's guitar playing gave us a unique identity which set us apart from every other band at the time. Another factor that made us so tight is that because we were in Texas, we got the chance to play long sets every night, maybe two or three hours, whereas in L.A. a band would get fifteen minutes. So if we fucked up, nobody cared and we knew we had another forty-five songs in the set to make up for it. At one point we played the Bronco Bowl in Dallas and it felt like it was something we were supposed to do.

———

Now that Darrell had started drinking, our relationship got stronger, and because I was spending a lot of time on his mom's couch, we'd hang out a lot, as friends, when we weren't playing gigs or practicing. While his brother Vinnie was asleep at night, Darrell and I would take Vinnie's car, a '69 Oldsmobile Cutlass, for a joy ride, and we'd call it, "Working it in big boy's car."

So we'd take this thing out on Monterrey Street and our thing in those days was to drive through people's lawns and then peel out so hard that they've got no fucking lawn left, known as a "lawn job." Laying the power down massively, taking out mail boxes, the whole fucking bit. The funny thing is that Vinnie never even knew we did it because we always put the car back in the same place for the next morning.

Dime and I used to fuck him over so bad it was stupid. Once, Dime and me drove to this gig way out of town in Shreveport, at least three and a half hours from Dallas. I'm hauling ass in that Cutlass going about ninety miles an hour, and by the time we'd gotten about halfway there, smoke is pouring out of this motherfucker from under the hood.

We pull over thinking it's the radiator, which it was. But it was not only that because I knew I had already blown the heads in it on a previous lawn-shredding outing. So we open it up and this old guy comes over and shouts at the top of his voice, "Hey boys, stand back! You're fixin' to get burned!" This guy was straight out of *Green Acres*, the epitome of how people talk, and I can still hear that guy's voice in my head today. "Fixin'" is a real local expression by the way, meaning that you're about to do something or something's about to happen, and I use the term all the time.

"Hang on, I'll be right over there!" this old guy says, and when he comes over, he slowly takes his cap off, and then *boom*, the radiator blows. Vinnie's Cutlass wouldn't be going anywhere. We had to find a phone booth out in the middle of nowhere and call someone who was going to the gig and tell them what had happened so they could come out and get us.

BECAUSE OF OLD MAN Abbott's clout in the local music scene at the time, he could take us three to blues clubs to watch these blues legends who formed part of the resurgence of the late '70s and early '80s, a band called Savvy, for example, who had their own grimy club downtown where your shoes would stick to the carpet.

He knew all these people because he'd done sessions with them, so we'd go along and watch how things are done, how to perform live and the whole bit. It wasn't a Rock 'n' Roll 101 course or anything like that, it was more a case of just going out and watching these cats jam. Even though Arlington was still a relatively small town, it still had a population of maybe two hundred and fifty thousand, so it was a whole lot bigger than the peanut town I came from, and consequently a much bigger pool of musical talent. These guys we went to see play were definitely some of the coolest dudes in town, and when you're in your late teens—thinking about rock 'n' roll and that whole darker type of image—these cats were just what I needed, because I definitely knew I didn't want to play fucking Journey covers for the rest of my life.

TERRY GLAZE

Because we spent so much time around musicians and performers as teenagers, Darrell and Vinnie lived the rock star lifestyle from this very early age and it wasn't an act: they actually lived it out twenty-four hours a day. They didn't turn it off. I always wanted to be a performer who could go and do my show, and then come off and be a different person, but they were that person *all the time*. Kind of like the persona of a wrestler, you could say.

———

During the process of all the playing gigs and hanging out in local clubs, we continued to have pretty much free reign in the studio if the old man wasn't booked, so we used that time to get the material down for these early records, which we sold from the trunks of cars or between sets of our live shows. Our debut *Metal Magic* came out in '83—produced by the old man in his own Pantego Sound studio— with either Jerry or Darrell coming up with the ideas for songs.

All we did was practice and write songs, so it's no surprise that by the time we were eighteen we were as tight a live band as you could get. It was all new to us, having the freedom to use Jerry Abbott's studio, and it was so exciting. Someone would say, "The studio is free next Thursday, let's go!" It was a great training ground for all of us to learn our craft. Some bands have goals to be the best band at their high school or the best band in their city; we never thought like that. We always thought that one of these days we'll be on tour with Van Halen. We didn't want to be the local band, we wanted to be the biggest band in the world, and so our vision was much bigger than most other bands. We played the Bronco Bowl in Dallas one time and it just seemed like that was what we were supposed to do. We even had a full-blown stage show produced by a guy we called "Pyro" who—you guessed it—did pyrotechnics. We didn't reserve the big show for special occasions either, we did it every night.

Then we just *kept* writing songs, either in the old man's studio or we'd rent a warehouse somewhere to rehearse in until we got kicked out. As well as rehearsing and playing gigs, I was also the kind of guy who liked hanging out at the lake. I was a lake person. I'd get out there and throw Frisbees, pick up hot chicks and the whole bit. Everybody wanted to jam at six o clock on Sundays, so I'd always show up full of booze after spending the day at the lake.

I suppose I felt like I didn't really need to practice and that the only reason I thought I was there was for everyone else in the room's benefit. Learning something new took me no time at all. I did it all by ear and knew all the notes. But I always feared that despite my natural ability, my reluctance to rehearse might just make the brothers turn round one day and say, "Okay, we've had enough." They lived to practice. I didn't. I lived to enjoy myself and play music while doing so, so there was a potential conflict.

Thankfully, it never came to that, and in 1984 we did our second record, *Projects in the Jungle*, again produced by the old man in his studio. Of all our early stuff, I really dig this one. We were evolving as musicians and *Projects* was exploring the direction where we wanted to go and also provided a big, upward learning curve. It was mostly all our own compositions, but occasionally the old man would bring a song in for us, and we'd just adapt what he had to fit our own version of what we wanted to do, so he was entitled to some songwriting royalties for some of these earlier tunes. I mention this only because royalties would be an issue later on down the line.

Although I didn't initially make the connection, my newfound business know-how helped. I was also doing everything I could to learn about the business side of the music industry, in order to minimize the chances of getting screwed over in the future. Because even I knew that getting fucked—usually by your manager—came with the territory of being a musician.

So whenever I had spare time sitting in the studio I read *Billboard* magazine and any interesting music industry–related book I could get my hands on, articles that told you how to protect yourself and the whole bit. Every musician needs to know the kind of stuff I was reading, how all the pie charts work when it comes to songwriting credit. I actually think it really pissed off the old man because he knew I was fucking learning a lot, and maybe stuff he didn't want me to know, too. He even started calling me "The Lawyer."

While our live performances became steadily tighter and more accomplished, musically the band was becoming influenced by different shit, too. Even though our material still had a loose, pop sensibility to it, the riffs were steadily getting harder and heavier. Listening to Metallica back in '83 and '84, *Ride the Lightning* changed everything and so began a whole new step in the evolution of heavy metal. Their first record had turned our heads in a heavier direction, but the progression to *Ride the Lightning* was huge and certainly influenced our next studio recording, *I Am the Night*, released in 1985.

TERRY GLAZE

We all drove to see Metallica play in some college in Tyler, Texas one time. We even wore our spandex! It was like playing in a big cafeteria and we ended up booking a show in that same room at some point in the future. I was the only one with a credit card, and the next morning I found out that everything had been put on my card. We also did a show in Houston playing with Megadeth, and I think that they actually approached Darrell to go and join their band but Darrell wouldn't go if Vinnie wasn't included in the deal, which is kind of ironic given that in high school it was Darrell who was the throw-in on the trade package!

———

Sure, we were getting into heavier music but we still knew that the only way to get gigs locally was still to dress up—hair sticking up near the ceiling and the whole fucking bit—and appease the club crowd, because these were the people that were allowing us to survive. You could argue that our early look stifled our progress to some degree, but the counterbalance was that it allowed us to be seen by many more people than we might otherwise have been. Definitely a good tradeoff in retrospect, and we always put on the best show we possibly could.

WHEN METALLICA'S *Master of Puppets* came out in '86, I remember being completely blown away by it when we listened to it for the first time at the Abbott house. They had a pretty nice turntable in there and goddamn it we played that record over and over again while I just sat on the couch in awe. Metallica still had a melodic sense and they also wrote really great, complex songs, whereas with Slayer—who would also get popular in '85 and '86—we looked at that and said, "Yeah, well that's cool, but not really the direction we want to go."

TERRY GLAZE

We were all listening to Van Halen, Def Leppard, and stuff like that, but Darrell and Rex were the ones that discovered Metallica and they started going in that direction. I kind of followed but I felt with that kind of music, the guitar was the hook and the vocals were secondary. I liked songs that you could wash your car to where the vocals were the hook, but the band direction was going away from that to a place where the song was driven primarily by guitar hooks. I thought the strongest songs we did were where Darrell and I combined. He might take one of my songs and make the guitar parts better but generally our sound got progressively heavier as a wider range of bands influenced us.

———

We saw Metallica when they supported Raven in '83 or '84, but never got a chance to meet them. Rita Haney—a chick who was always hanging around Dime—did know them, so then in '85, when they came back through town with W.A.S.P and Armored Saint, we got to hang out with them. I remember being completely in awe of them and their music because they were doing exactly what we hoped we could do. That experience really had a big impact on me and Dime in particular. Even at that time Hetfield was the kind of guy who you just *let* talk—very, very serious and you got the sense that there was something grilling upstairs but you were never sure what it was.

But he and Lars let Dime and I jam with them at Savvy's on a few songs from their first record, and from that point the friendship was set. Let's just say that jamming on some Metallica tracks with these guys made me think that we, too, could reach that kind of level and break out of the Texas scene into something way bigger. They were our idols, and remember, they were nowhere near the band they would become when they really blew up. But even at this stage they had a street-wise attitude to being on the road that we really admired and the various levels of debauchery that it involved.

They had a chick in every town that they nicknamed "the Edna's"—someone they were fucking on every trip—and because we knew an "Edna" in our town, that was our standing joke with them from that point on.

We also ran into Marc Ferrari of Keel at a show somewhere, and when he heard our demo tape he went on this mission to help promote us with a view to getting us signed. That's how we got the word around. It really stuck with him and whenever he had a break from tour he'd take a two-week sabbatical to help us out. His enthusiasm really put a foot in the door for us whenever we went out to L.A., because he knew all these guys like Tommy Thayer and the guys from Black 'n Blue. Ferrari would make sure he handed out plenty of our cassettes so that our music was heard by as many people as possible. Distribution was the issue with the early records. Yes we had an importer trying to get the word out there but because the records were produced independently, they were expensive for the fans to get a hold of; but despite that we still managed to move around 25,000 copies of *I Am the Night*.

ME, A BLIND DATE, and Rita Haney were all fixin' to go up to San Francisco to try to hang out with the Metallica boys. So we rented a car and set off—Dime, who was still pretty brand-new when it came to being away from home, ended up chickening out, leaving me and the two girls to go up to San Francisco without him. We never made contact with the Metallica guys, but we hung out a few days, took a bunch of drugs, and I puked all over every inch of Golden Gate State Park. I still have the photographs to prove it.

We also got to see a record dealer called Import Exchange, who handled the import and export of our records up until that point. They already handled other metal artists like Metallica and Anthrax, but the purpose of going in person to see them was simply to say, "Here I am; what have you done for me lately?" Otherwise it's hard to know whether they're actually doing anything for you or not. Luckily it seemed that they *had* actually done something because we were starting to see a little bit of cash from record sales coming in.

When we got back, we needed to make a decision on who was going to be the band's singer going forward. Terry Glaze was a pretty good songwriter, had that high voice and the hooks, but that wasn't the direction we were going in. He was also trying to finish his college and we were kind of tired of him trying to be fucking Dave Lee Roth, so we needed a replacement. Dime did this thing with Terry where he'd leave a boot in his guitar case as if to say, "I gave him the boot," but Terry never did work out what it meant.

TERRY GLAZE

I was attending college while I was still in the band, so one thing wasn't affecting the other at that time, but I was getting tired of the way that the business structure of the band was playing out, and I knew that was going to be an issue later on. The Abbott's had three votes—the old man and the brothers and they would never ever split their vote on *anything*—so I knew I was never ever going to have any say on band issues. So if my commitment could be questioned near the end it was because of that and the fact that I didn't really like the super-heavy direction it looked like we were headed in. The last night we played together was in Shreveport, Louisiana, and it was a very strange end. We got up onstage, played a great show and then afterwards, that was it. No "Hey, man, all the best" or anything; we just parted ways.

———

We tried out a bunch of other guys as singers for a few months but none of them were what we wanted, until a booking agent of ours suggested we get in touch with a guy called Phil Anselmo out of a band called Razor White, a metal band who'd been out touring like we had but with more emphasis on states like Mississippi. Vinnie got him on the phone a couple times and then said to us, "Look, I've been talking to this guy and we've got to at least try him out. He sounds really cool; he's got this Bon Jovi–type pitch to him." To which I thought, "Oh, fuck."

It was a couple of weeks before Christmas in 1986 and we still had shows to play that year, one of them on New Year's Eve in Shreveport. So I talked to Phil on the phone and we all agreed that he should fly out and try out for the band.

By now I had moved from my position on the Abbott couch and was living in a place with a bunch of drug dealers who were raking in so much cash I didn't have to pay them any rent. They had an extra bedroom and were buying us equipment as well, kind of like sponsors, so if things worked out with Phil, he'd have a place to stay right away. I should say that I had no part in their drug business; I just lived high on the hog with the money it was bringing in.

RITA HANEY

Rex had spent a lot of those early days at Darrell and Vinnie's house, sleeping on the couch, and their mom Carolyn definitely saw Rex as their third son. His mother was sick and his father had died at a really early age, so he didn't really have a lot of family in his life, except the boys and their mom.

———————

On the day Phil was due to arrive in town, one of the guys I was living with loaned me his bright red '77 Corvette Stingray so I could go and pick Phil up at the airport, and that definitely made an impression. I wanted it to turn his head. Phil must have definitely thought, "Wow, this is a fucking trip."

We took Phil and his bags to the house and told him this is where he'd be staying for a little bit (which ended up being two years), then that night I took him to rehearse in the front room of mama Abbott's house. Vinnie and Dime's folks had been divorced since back when the boys were in junior high, so they lived with their mother Carolyn in a small place in Arlington that became Pantera headquarters. We kept all our stuff in the garage and we had also bought a trailer, and I'd have girls over and bang them in there, which was kind of cool back then.

So, that first night with Phil we set up a PA, where we had a bottle of tequila—my drink of choice at the time—and a joint, and jammed like we'd been together for an eternity. Everything clicked right off the bat. Phil had just turned eighteen.

CHAPTER 6

THE KID FROM
THE BIG EASY

Eighteen or not, Phil Anselmo was a bad ass. Even at that age he was the kind of guy that you knew the moment he walked in the room not to fuck with him. He and I stayed in the drug dealer's house for two years until it became too hot. The cops eventually came and busted the place, thankfully after we'd both moved out. I moved in with my girlfriend, Elena, who was becoming my first real love, and Phil shared a place with some other friends but he always had that chip on his shoulder—something to prove all the time—and he would never back away from a confrontation.

One night we were playing at Savvy's club, which was still our regular gig, and a guy from some other band shouted his mouth off at Phil. Phil went outside and kicked the *whole* band's ass without any help. That's the kind of guy he was. He was a fuckin' bruiser. Being from New Orleans and us being from Dallas meant that Phil immediately brought a new dynamic into the band. He'd had a different upbringing than we'd had in Texas, so he definitely brought the tough guy street smarts, and he was also as funny as hell. Really, really intelligent. The cat is brilliant at what he does. Even then he was one of the best writers I'd ever seen.

He'd been raised mainly by his stepfather and was heavily into horror movies from a very young age. Then metal caught his attention—it really turned him around. Back then he had this incredible, high voice. He could sing Rob Halford stuff and just nail it, and that's what we were into because we felt that the high stuff would go great with all the riffing happening downstairs.

As part of our efforts to get noticed, we went to Hollywood and showcased our material everywhere—the Whisky, Troubadour, and Gazzarri's—every place that we could possibly get in. Then we had a residency for a week in Phoenix and one in El Paso, Texas, trying to make enough bread just so we could put fuel in the vehicle and get back home. Whatever my kitty was from playing all these sets for a week, my bar tab pretty much took me out of the picture, even though I was still underage. It was pretty tight living.

! # ⊕ *

SO WITH GIGS taking up nights and weekends, we'd spend the days just writing songs. The boys would get me and Phil, and we'd all go to the studio and start piecing stuff together. We probably already had two-thirds of the *Power Metal* record done by this point—certainly we had all the melodies—but Phil started turning us on to all kinds of different stuff that we hadn't listened to before, because he turned out to be the biggest fucking metalhead of all time. He knew every fucking band there was to know.

Thrash metal was the big thing at the time, with bands like Anthrax, Metallica, Megadeth, and Slayer all releasing killer thrash metal records in '86 and '87, and it seemed that if you didn't have some kind of thrash element to your songs you were going to be left behind.

As closed-minded as the Abbott brothers were, they *listened* to the stuff that Phil put on in the vehicle and it would make a really big impact. They had no choice anyway. When we were driving, Phil was always in the front seat being the DJ and so bands like Voivod, Venom, Soundgarden, and a lot of Mercyful Fate—that kind of stuff—appeared on our radar and definitely influenced how we viewed our own sound, even if it only registered on a subliminal level. None of it was mainstream and nobody at any of the places we normally played would have known any of these band's songs, but Phil's more hardcore background was inadvertently steering us on to a much more extreme path.

Logically, with most of *Power Metal* already done, we decided to scratch the existing vocals and let Phil do what he did. As a result, and in contrast to what everyone likes to say, *Power Metal* is much heavier than anything we'd done before.

By this time we had bought a Ryder truck, had more gear, and also had a full-blown road crew working for us, so Vince and I used to take the old man's car, a decrepit Pontiac Grand Prix, to gigs. Vince couldn't drive to save his life and he always wanted to tow his boat behind the car when we went on the road, so that we could stop somewhere and go fishing. He would just *run over* shit and that boat would come off the back all the time, and we'd have to say to him, "Vince, look how the boat's sitting now." And it would be sitting sideways or backwards or something.

"Ohhh shit, well Goddamn; then I better roll it over!" That's how Vinnie talks.

"Yeah that would be nice, if you want to keep the boat and save it," I'd say. We then had to tie the boat down on the trailer so that it wouldn't come off while Vinnie was driving.

We used that boat to do a lot of fishing and caught a shitload of bass. I remember we got lost once out in some body of water and Vinnie kept trying to direct us.

"Take a right. Take a right here," he'd shout.

"Vince, you have no fucking idea where we are. It's dark." And there were these big stumps that stood up two feet out of the water, which of course we hit and the boat almost turned over many times. He was a bad-ass fucking drummer but a complete liability in many other ways, I'll tell you.

! ⌗ ⊕ *

WHEN WE WEREN'T GETTING LOST in the boat, Pantera was starting to gather this incredible fan base in town. We'd sell out every night and start making some pretty good dough playing places like the Basement, Joe's Garage, Matlock's, Dallas City Limits, and, of course, Savvy's.

This was during what seemed to be a whole movement where people were getting into m-e-t-a-l music instead of pop-rock like Bon Jovi (we *never* covered their songs)—they even had to remodel Joe's Garage to fit more people, and that became our home court. Yes, we still had the big, wild hair at the time, but that was just to look the part and get a foot in the door. Musically we were headed somewhere else, although I should mention that I definitely got more chicks wearing spandex and shit than I ever did after I started wearing simple shorts and a shirt.

So while our constant live presence was attracting a large local fan base, it was also grabbing the attention of other metal bands that came through town, which helped get our name out there. One night while Slayer were in town on the *South of Heaven* tour, they showed up at one of our gigs on a night off, and by the time the night was over, Kerry and Tom got on stage and started jamming on "Reign in Blood" with us. Next thing I know, Phil and Kerry are best buddies and Kerry's sleeping on Phil's couch. At one point I even thought that Kerry wanted to join the fucking band. That's how intense it was.

Power Metal came out in '88, our first album with Phil on vocals, and although a lot of people like to say that we were playing a glam style of music, I think that's a total misconception. Although the image we portrayed may have *looked* like other hair bands, the music we were playing was much heavier and showed more of a thrash metal influence from bands like Slayer and Metallica. It was still funded by all of us—we paid for all the studio time at Pantego Studio produced by the old man. We all felt this need to move our career up to the next step because we were still selling records and merchandise from the back of the car, which was very DIY non-professional.

Despite that, the record would go on to sell a hard-to-ignore 40,000 copies on Metal Magic Records—our own independent label—and it was no surprise when the major labels started looking closely after that. With the import guys up in San Francisco and another importer moving the record for us, we finally started seeing some decent cash come in.

Having label interest, which we had, and actually having a record deal are two different things. Something that definitely hadn't helped us actually *secure* a major record deal was that we had a really shitty lawyer, even though Jerry Abbott really thought he'd hit the fuckin' jackpot when he found the guy.

The way I see it, the real reason old man Abbott hired him was that he could mislead the dude and secure the rights to some of our early publishing and later, our *major* publishing. It was soon clear to us that this guy was no good, kind of washed up, and he definitely wasn't getting the point across as to what Pantera was all about. We kept telling Jerry that we had to change something—get another lawyer—because this guy wasn't doing fucking anything for us, but looking back it seems clear that he had his own reasons for leaving things as they were.

The frustration was getting to us. We already had demos for what would later become *Cowboys from Hell,* had the thing pretty much in the can, and here we were trying to live this dream but the rejection began to get really monotonous. Every major label we talked to said the same thing: "No, we drop." "No, we'll pass." "No, we can't do this." "Send us more material"—every excuse you can think of. We seemed to be getting nowhere while our peers were going everywhere.

Case in point, Metallica—who were roughly our age—would soon be out playing stadiums with Van Halen, but before they did, they came through town again while they were in the studio recording ... *And Justice for All.* Every time we got together with these guys, it just got dumber and dumber. We'd go out with them to a strip bar, and Lars would just pick someone out and say, "This is on *your* tab." We barely had money to buy cigarettes, far less huge drink rounds. We were all still surviving on two hundred bucks a week at this time, and I remember going out to a tit bar with these guys and it was seven bucks a shot.

"Dude, we're all fucking broke," I told him, when his finger finally pointed in my direction to pay a tab which included several rounds of shots.

"This round is on *you!*" Lars said again, so Dime and I just walked out the door of this tit bar and left Vinnie sitting there.

On another one of these nights we were sitting outside some club and they were playing us their new record; there's no bass on it and they're laughing their asses off saying: "We got this new guy Jason and we're fucking with him—we're just not going to put his bass in the mix." They were fucking *howling* about it and I guess they saw it as their way of harassing him.

I'm saying, "So where's the bass?" and they just said, "Ha ha, it's not on it." There's been a lot of debate and speculation about that issue over the years as to whether it was an intentional attempt to humiliate Jason Newsted, and we heard it straight from their mouths. They meant it.

HEAVY MUSIC WAS really changing in '89. It seemed like there was this whole different brand of music appearing on the horizon that'd soon be labeled Alternative: the first Jane's Addiction record, the live one; Faith No More; Voivod; and Soundgarden—all these kinds of bands who put out crushing records. So we absorbed these influences along with what we'd taken from what Metallica had done, and created our own thing.

CHAPTER 7

WE'RE TAKING OVER THIS TOWN

Mark Ross, an A&R guy who worked for Atco Records, was stuck in town sometime in the fall of '89 because of Hurricane Hugo, so he decided to see us play. His boss, Derek Shulman, had already shown an interest in signing us, but he needed to know what we were all about live, so this seemed like a good opportunity to send one of his employees to see Pantera firsthand, and he certainly picked an unusual night.

We were playing a private birthday party in some strip mall in Dallas—certainly not our regular scene—and by the time we started playing, we'd all taken ecstasy. When Mark Ross turned up, the chick whose birthday it was had slipped on the birthday cake and there was icing all over the floor, and we were sliding around and dancing in it trying to have fun. Being on X makes you do goofy shit like that.

Mark had seen that we didn't take things too seriously. We wanted it to be badass shit, of course, and we took it seriously *enough*, but in between songs we were cut-ups and threw cake at each other like a bunch of classroom clowns.

Just a few minutes after showing up, Mark Ross left the place, at which point I turned to Vinnie and said, "He split, the dude's gone." After so many rejections, we were used to this same shit: rejection and people leaving. But then he came back.

The long and short of it is that over the next few months a bidding war would erupt over who was going to sign Pantera. Atco wanted us bad, and at the same time we were thinking about going with Roadrunner, but sometime in December Darrell turned up at my door holding a record contract from Atco Records, part of the Warner Music Group. That opened the door for us to go into the studio to record our first major label record *Cowboys from Hell*, a title that Phil came up with and which in all our minds suggested a kind of southern menace.

Our mentality was clear from the lyrics of the title track: "We're taking over this town." We felt like saying, "Here we are. Fuck you, and we're going to destroy you, so if you don't like it, fucking leave." This was the kind of attitude we cultivated to survive. We were all, as individuals and a group, very single-minded and strong-willed about what we wanted to do and where we wanted to go.

CHERYL PONDER

Mother was so proud of Rex when they signed a contract and of course she was so pleased that it was finally going to work out. But it wasn't without a lot of sleeping on other people's couches, particularly when he hadn't been getting along with her. She was relieved that his decision to pursue music had finally paid off.

But understand this beyond a doubt: neither Jerry Abbott nor the idiot lawyer got us that record deal, but the lawyer certainly collected his fee, you can guarantee that. It was *our* hard work, dedication, and word of mouth that got us the break we deserved. Despite this, Jerry Abbott made sure he would collect ridiculous royalties on the back of our hard work. So I was really pissed that despite having signed our first major label deal, we were still getting shortchanged. Yeah, that happened to pretty much every band, I guess, but I was bummed out we were not the exception to that rule despite my best efforts to be as clued-in as much as possible about how the business side of things worked.

As part of the Atco deal, we also started a management relationship with Walter O'Brien and his Concrete Management Company that would guide us until the band disbanded in 2003.

WALTER O'BRIEN (Pantera's former manager)

The band had reached out to me during the *Power Metal* days, well before the Atco deal, but I never really followed through on it at the time because they were basically a very different band. I had a connection with Atco because I'd gotten Metal Church out of their deal with Elektra and brought them to him. To cut a long story short, he didn't want them but he did want Pantera, and he wanted me to manage them. I wasn't all that thrilled and Derek said, "Yeah, but you haven't heard this?" and he was referring of course to the *Cowboys from Hell* demo tapes. I was blown away and it sounded like the future of heavy metal. Mark Ross, who had seen them already, tried to get me to come down to Texas to see them live, and I hesitated for a few days. The night he was leaving he called me again and said, "Look, it's your last chance, I'm leaving now for the airport and if you leave now you can still make it. If you don't like

them, I'll pick up your airfare and your hotel bill." I said,
"You know what, I don't have anything else to do and if
you're that serious, what the hell." So I went down there
and met him and the band beforehand at a place called
Dallas City Limits, and the band was funny. The first thing
Rex said was, "We want you to come onstage to do a cover
of 'Green Manalishi'!" He was totally kidding of course,
but when I saw this band come out onstage and explode,
I'd never seen anything like it. Rex and Dime were like
alternating jumping as high as they could; Phil was
climbing up the drum kit and flying in the air and by
the second or third song I was literally on my knees at
the side of the stage saying, "Please let me manage you."
I wouldn't say we did a handshake deal but as far as I was
concerned it was just a matter of paperwork. I was in.
If they didn't want me, that was another story.

Other than the fact that we were still using his studio, the old man
was now frozen out of the deal. He was no longer our manager nor
was he our producer, as Terry Date had been approached to look after the production after Phil and I had really gotten into what he did
with Soundgarden's *Louder Than Love* record. But Terry wasn't our
first choice or even our second.

PRONG HAD JUST put out a record called *Beg to Differ*, produced by
Mark Dodson, and we all really loved the tone of it but we couldn't
get ahold of Mark for some reason. Then we thought about Max
Norman, who did the Ozzy records, so he came down. Max was cra-
zier than a fucking loon, drinking all the time, and he had this lazy
eye so you never knew who or what the fuck he was looking at.

WALTER O'BRIEN

Max was going to produce this record, but his manager Ron Laffitte, who was a good friend of mine, kept dragging his feet and everyone wanted to get going into the studio right away. Here's the thing: I knew that Max was holding out to produce a much bigger band than Pantera, but Max's manager didn't know I knew that. While all the delays with Max were going on, I told the Pantera guys about Terry Date because I managed him also. So I suggested Terry go down for the weekend to see how it goes with the condition that if Max got back to me, Terry would have to step down. I did hear from Max's manager—three days after he was meant to call me—but by that time we'd agreed that Terry was the guy, and in retrospect I don't think Max and Pantera would have been a good match; they'd have been trading blows within minutes—and I love Max!

————

When Terry Date came down he fit in perfectly. He was hungry, kind of middle class like us, really knew his shit, smoked weed, and didn't really drink that much—which was good because we needed someone to be in control and, more important, keep us in control. We used to say, "Terry, produce me a beer!" It was his job to make sure there was just enough beer in the studio.

TERRY DATE (Pantera's producer)

I really have no idea about who in the band requested me but I got involved because my ex-manager—who I'd left six months earlier—called me up and said he had a demo tape from this band from Texas that he really wanted me to listen to, which was *Cowboys from Hell*. I listened, really loved it, and flew down to meet them in Dallas. To my recollection they knew pretty much everything by then and when I came in they were very organized except for maybe a couple of songs. Rex, Vinnie, and Dime would work out the stuff first of all, and then Phil would come in and make sure it fit into his world. That's how they worked. I never felt limited by one guitar player and one bass player either; in fact when it's that guitar player and that bass player it's actually a luxury.

———————

Pantego Sound is located in a little subdivision section of town just outside of Arlington, and when you walk in the door there are parquet floors everywhere. There's a drum room on one side of the building and a huge main room, so we started by putting nothing but eight by ten plywood sections on the main room floor. We wanted to get it as bright and lively as we possibly could, but we felt that the room was kind of dead. It had to be right because, for a record that needed to clearly demonstrate our aggressive intentions, we desperately wanted that "attack" kind of feel.

This was long before the days of Pro Tools or anything like that, so our approach was to play everything live on the floor, often without Phil's vocals. So, if you wanted to play with a bass cabinet, which I mostly did, you still had to baffle stuff off with a 4 × 4 piece of wood or fiberglass—both of which serve to reflect the sound. Nowadays you wouldn't have to do that, of course. Technology can get around that. You can just plug into a pod (basically a pre-amp) that modulates the sound and then sends the signal wherever you want it to go.

We'd all play on the floor while Vinnie was getting his drum track done, and just about every first take he did was the best. But because he was such a perfectionist, he usually ended up with twenty different drum tracks that he would endlessly analyze and say, "Well, I like how that part felt better there; let's put that in there."

Then he wouldn't like that so they'd have to chop it back and forth while Dime and I would just be sitting there going, "Dude, this is fucking taking forever." Vinnie's drum tracks are what took most of our time in the studio. Plus, with a multi-reel recording system like we had, you actually had to physically cut tape with a razor blade, and know exactly where you cut it, then connect other pieces of tape together so that you can run it back and forth. It was a nightmare unless you happened to get it right on, and because Vinnie and Dime wanted to be so precise and technical, it would get to the point where we ran out of fucking razor blades and tape.

Because Vinnie had spent so much time in the studio with his old man as a kid, he was very technical-minded and already had a pretty good ear for what the sound was going to be like for the drums and guitar at least. But he didn't know shit about bass and, back in the day, bass sounds weren't really very noticeable anyway, particularly on heavy metal records. Because of our set-up, with only one guitar player with a huge sound like Darrell had, bass was an important feature of the makeup, albeit a real dipped sound (when the voltage output dips at high volume causing the sound to be compressed) that really added to the kick-drum. Bass was still sonically there, but it was always so hard to fit in with Darrell's guitar. He always played with a little solid-state amp behind him and his signal path was fucking ridiculous.

I remember thinking his whole sound was just so overpowering. We often joked that if somebody else plugged into Darrell's rig they could never sound like him. But if Darrell plugged into any other gear, he would always sound like himself. He was that unique.

His brother's drums were overpowering, too, but for different reasons. Vinnie liked a lot of reverb because that was another sonic trend he had learned from his old man. There was an echo chamber underneath the drum platform and it was this huge spring that he loved the sound of, but sometimes I felt that it bordered on overshadowing the fucking song.

Dime always wanted me to play every riff pretty much as he did—sort of mirror it an octave lower—but as a trained jazz bass player, I wanted to incorporate more of an "okay, if you're going to play way up high, we need someone on the bottom who's going to syncopate with what you're doing upstairs" type of thing. That was a major thought in the back of my mind. I didn't want to always play what I played, but I was conscious of the fact that it's easy, as a bass player, to step all over the melody. I just wanted a balance.

So while we all had a sense of what we wanted our individual parts to sound like, Terry Date's job was to put it all together in a way that didn't sound like four individual people, but like a tight-as-fuck band.

With most iconic records there's always a moment that ignites the process, and ours was when Dime came up with the signature riff for the track "Cowboys from Hell" completely out of the blue. Of course at first we said, "What the fuck is this?" But as we gave it time and lived with it while driving around in the car for a couple of days, we realized it had this groove to it that suddenly gave us our own sound, something that we weren't even conscious of trying to do. We just wanted to write the best songs we could and sequence them in such a way that would make a killer record, but this type of groove took us by surprise.

Technically, *Cowboys'* title track is one of those box riffs, because you're playing inside of a box. What I mean is that it's basically a blues scale, something we'd all probably picked up on from watching all these blues players in the clubs with the old man. Sure, Darrell could play all the other scales he wanted—scales you've never even fucking heard of, too—but if you really listened to what his essence was, you're hearing a lot of blues, just at a faster tempo.

Terry Date was very smart because whenever anyone was in the room, he'd have tape rolling. So even if we were just sitting there fucking with a riff and not doing anything formal, he would always be recording so that we could go back at a later date and listen to what we had. Back then we couldn't afford to roll two-inch tape—or at least not like someone like Tom Petty, who does it from the moment he walks in the studio—but we'd always have *something* rolling, even if it was just a basic cassette, so we could go back and say, "let's try this part" or "let's change that part" as we built new tracks.

"Cemetery Gates" was written while Dime and I sat in the office playing on acoustic guitars, mine being some big, orange Kramer acoustic bass that someone had bought me. He had the major riff already worked out but the intro part was all me and him, and I ended up playing acoustic guitar and piano in the finished song, which added a little texture.

We pretty much just jammed through all the songs to get a feel for them and make sure the formula was right—the bridge was here and the chorus was there and the whole bit. Then we'd get down to the lead section and say, "Okay, Jesus Christ, what the fuck are we going to do here? Do we change chords?" But we could always work it out.

"Primal Concrete Sledge" was one of the few songs that we didn't have written and demoed before we got in the studio. It came off a drum pattern that Vinnie had and then the riff was built around it. Then we'd go section by section until it was all done, rough, punching everything on tape like some kind of Frankenstein's monster. Then we made a copy and drove around listening to it for a day or two and that was the way that we decided if we were happy with what we'd come up with.

Getting the lyrics down for the record worked out pretty easily, too. We'd just give Phil the riff and he'd listen to the song and pretty much come back the next day with something. He'd ask for a few words or notes every once in a while, but the rest of it he did himself because, in that sense, he's a genius. He was *always* writing. There was always a notepad and pen in his hands, and when he wasn't doing anything else, he was writing ideas for songs and always took it, and everything else happening, very seriously.

I remember one night while we were making *Cowboys* when Phil came into the studio crying like a baby. His buddy Mike Tyson had gone down in Tokyo. Basically it looked like Tyson had gone over there, did a bunch of blow, didn't train, and got his ass kicked. Well, for Phil it was like the world had ended.

"Fuck you all. Fuck every one of you motherfuckers," I think he said.

"Dude, it's a fucking boxing match," I told him. Then I just sat there and laughed at how something so trivial matters so much to someone.

WALTER O'BRIEN

I was in and out of the studio while they did the record but only to listen and be excited about it and not to tell my band how to make a record. If I knew how to do that, I'd be making records myself! I trusted them and I trusted Terry, so I would just go in every couple of weeks just to make sure it was headed in the right direction. If I had problems, I'd let them know, but I never really had any problems.

———

Because we'd been organized and had everything demoed well in advance, *Cowboys from Hell* was probably done in a couple of months. We were already starting to go up to New York to showcase the band at places like L'Amour and the Cotton Club before the record was even mixed at the Carriage House in Connecticut. Going to our first real big mix was a trip, too, seeing how that all went down. At the end of the day we were all just bawling like kids saying, "Wow, what an awesome record." And so at last *Cowboys* was ready to go and so were we.

Our image was new and so was the music. So while I would always acknowledge the pre-*Cowboys* material as being an important part of my personal musical development, we, as a band did make a conscious decision to distance ourselves from those first four records.

We definitely wouldn't have been as insanely tight as we'd gotten without those tough formative years, nor would we've been as bombastic as live performers—we knew that—but when *Cowboys* came out we all decided, "Look, that was our past, let's let it be."

CHAPTER 8

EARLY TOURS AND ANECDOTES

Presumably to start immediately recouping their investment, Atco records wanted us out touring the record as
quickly as possible, so even before the record came out
in July 1990 we were out on the road in April, initially with Suicidal
Tendencies and Exodus. Now that we had a foot in the door, it was
time to start working.

WALTER O'BRIEN

I brought the band to a booking agent named John Ditmar,
and I knew he'd be the guy to organize this and between
us we used our contacts to get the band exposure.
Normally metal bands would go out for eight weeks and
then were done, but I said, "No, this band has got to work

every day of the week for at least a year because that's how you break a band." You've got to play small places first and work your way up, not because you're small, but because you want the fans to have that intimate connection—the kind that lasts a lifetime. So we'd tried to open for a bigger act but then we'd always go back and headline a smaller place and we rotated that; and we certainly weren't going to pull the plug after eight weeks. Instead they played two hundred and sixty-four dates touring *Cowboys from Hell* in the U.S. alone…

————

We rode in something that could only be described as a fucking bucket of bolts. This thing was like a mobile home and it never stopped moving, day after day, night after night, except for the eighteen or so times that the fucking thing broke down along the way. For a lot of the time we didn't even have working headlights, so one of us had to hold the wires together when we saw a vehicle coming in the opposite direction so that we'd be visible.

Forget beds, all you had to rest in was a chair that would lean back only just far enough to allow you to sleep on it. But you didn't sleep. It was cramped, there was too much noise and it was a hundred degrees. The only time it wasn't a hundred degrees was when it was a thousand degrees.

WHILE PHIL HAD UPPED his game significantly as a vocalist on the record, he was still trying to find himself as a front man, a true performer, so Suicidal Tendencies were great road mates for us. Mike Muir was a fucking huge influence on him, and I'm sure Phil would acknowledge that. Mike has this demeanor onstage that makes you not want to fuck with him, and Phil definitely wanted that same vibe.

He saw the respect that Mike got because of it, so that's where a lot of his tough guy front man shtick comes from for sure.

! # ⊕ *

DESPITE THE BRUTAL LACK of comforts, this was one of the best tours we ever did as far as exposure was concerned, and we were also able to keep things much more simple than they would become when we became a much bigger band.

Sound check? Forget it. Writing down a set list each night? Fuck that. We just got up there and fucking ripped.

In lots of ways it was a culture shock because it took us to cities that we'd never visited before—most we'd never even heard of—and that forced us to grow up real quick. None of us had ever really left the roost before and we had survived on short, touring trips around the Southwest, places no more than a few hours from home, before returning to the familiarity of Texas. This time it was different. We were fucking miles from home, but we were so psyched to be out there that it just didn't matter. "Fuck you all" was our approach. These motherfuckers were going to know that Pantera had been in their town, and we showed up in more than half of the fifty states and Canada while we were out on that first big tour.

While we were in Toronto, sometime before Christmas 1990, playing at a place called the Diamond Club, we caught the attention of Rob Halford, who saw us being interviewed—Dime wearing a *British Steel* t-shirt—on the TV in his hotel room. His band Judas Priest was also in town. I think he then contacted Darrell, came to the club, and next thing he's up playing "Metal Gods" and "Grinder" with us on stage, songs we used to play when we were doing covers in the Texas clubs.

Soon after that, an offer came to go to Europe with Judas Priest, on that leg of their Painkiller tour, and by this time we thought we were pretty good at touring. It was three months of us and Annihilator sharing a bus, and at that time nobody in Europe really knew who the fuck we were. But we didn't care. We were invincible and we would make them know who we were, right? We were eighteen swinging dicks on one bus, and it just wasn't fun. A couple of them got their asses kicked a few times, but we got along all right, mainly.

! # ⊕ *

PLAYING WITH PRIEST presented more problems than you would think because when you're opening for a band like them, crowds get antsy to see the main act: they throw bottles of piss and whatever and sometimes they don't give a shit about the support band, on principle. That wasn't the case with Pantera, though. More people got us than didn't. That's how Pantera were—we raged so hard and sounded so good, they had to like us.

We were also so damn lucky but were too young and gung-ho to even realize. Here we were, a bunch of dumb-ass kids out of Texas playing places in Europe like the K.B. Hallen in Copenhagen, where real bands had played before us—Zeppelin, the Beatles—you know, the really big league, man, about which I'd read in books like *Hammer of the Gods* and shit like that. I loved reading about the drama of rock 'n' roll bands and what they did on tour, so these places actually meant something to me.

! # ⊕ *

I JUST WISH I'd spent more time looking around all these towns—seeing significant landmarks and exploring the culture—instead of lying crashed-out in the hotel room, but you just don't see that at the time when you're young and new to the scene. Yes we wanted to take on the world when we were onstage, but we just didn't dig Europe at all; it was really foreign to us. We were so used to having pennies in our pockets and going down and getting bean burritos at the 7-11. That's basically the kind of shit we lived on: anything we could possibly afford. A sandwich here, a meal from some chick there, whatever, so it was really weird eating this food that we had never tasted before.

Here, they only gave us so many loaves of bread and so many pieces of cheese and meat; if you weren't up early, tough shit. Dime and I used to roll out of bed at 3 p.m. and everything would be fucking gone so we ended up just drinking beer instead.

Of course Dime and Vinnie just wanted their mom's franks and beans or their spaghetti cooked just like she normally cooked it, but you just don't get that over in Europe. Phil and I were a little more open-minded, but it still took a lot of adjustment. You can only eat chicken fucking cutlets so many times in Germany after all. It tastes like the same piece of shit that you had the day before, and it's the blandest-tasting food that you can ever eat. The same applies to England. I love shepherd's pie and fish 'n' chips, but is that all there is to fucking eat over there? Maybe I missed the other stuff or went to the wrong places, but there definitely seemed to be a lack of variety.

Although some aspects of the Priest tour were on a big scale because we were out with one of the biggest metal bands on the planet, don't think for a second that we were throwing money around. We hardly had any. Once we'd fixed food and done our laundry, there wasn't a whole lot left out of the fifteen-dollar-per-day allowance we were supposed to survive on. As always, there were perks here and there, but nothing major; we were always provided with beer for example, but we found out in the end that the truck driver had been fucking stealing it all for most of the tour so he truly got his ass kicked—almost lost his jaw and his eye sockets, and the whole fucking thing.

GUY SYKES (Pantera's tour manager)

The band invested their first advance check from Winterland [a huge merchandise company that had floated us twenty-five thousand dollars] on this tour, and this was back in the days when merch companies actually wrote advance checks, but they hated Europe. First of all there wasn't a lot of money. Secondly, the crews of older school bands didn't treat opening acts with much respect. So here we were: a bunch of guys who drank like we drank, and combine that with the fact that we were sharing a tour bus then, you can see how it was uncomfortable. In fact we only got two hotel rooms the whole three-month tour. The tour started in Copenhagen in the end of January 1991, so it was bitter cold and Europe pre the Euro. Different currency, different plugs, different everything so, from that aspect they didn't enjoy it.

———

Despite the fact they were a huge band that we totally looked up to, the Judas Priest guys were good to us and there's a reason for that. Not only did we respect them as our seniors, but we also were huge fans and had survived playing their stuff in the clubs, so to us it was like a dream come true to be out touring with them. Me and Phil played Ping-Pong with K. K. Downing and Glenn Tipton every night and they would fucking kill us; those guys were good. It was weird playing Ping-Pong with your idols, but we soon realized that they were just regular guys, and totally full of shit. We didn't see a whole lot of Rob Halford, though, he was pretty reclusive. But because Scott Travis was the only American in the band, we hung out with him a lot.

GUY SYKES

Judas Priest was one of several bands that Pantera toured with that they genuinely looked up to, so from that point of view the boys were like kids in a candy store. Pantera got along with everyone, simply because they'd spent so much of their early career entertaining the bar crowd, so they were always in a party mood.

———————

! # ⊕ *

DURING THE THREE-MONTH touring schedule, there were a few days in between where we had the chance to spend some down time together, which was something we had never done before. Vinnie and I got into playing a lot of golf, and whenever we had some time, we'd find a nice golf course and go play. That became our escape in future years, and as we earned more money, the stakes for these golf games with Vinnie and some of the crew just kept getting higher.

I have no idea who came up with this idea, but we decided to take a skiing trip on a day off—because Priest were on a night off or something that night, as I recall—and headed to the Swiss Alps. Now, I had been a good skier since I was ten or eleven years old, so I had no problem whatsoever with the whole deal, but none of the other guys had even been on skis before, and they had no fucking clue what they were doing.

Guy Sykes and I were the only two who could ski, and it was going to be a tough task to educate these guys how to just stay upright—far less anything else.

The first sign that the trip had been ill advised was when our sound guy Aaron Barnes—we called him "Johnny Ace"—could hardly put his skis on and when he did he hit a tree before he even got to the ski lift.

Holy shit, was this the level of uselessness that I was going to have to deal with?

Yep. And it would get a lot worse. I'm still amazed nobody died.

Somehow I got allocated the shitty job. My responsibility was to teach Dime and Philip to ski, which left Sykes to help Vinnie out. Without getting too technical, I wanted to try to explain how important the outside and inside edges of the skis were for stopping. Dime seemed to get the idea almost straight away because he used to ride skateboards and he had the feel and balance. A couple of rounds of coaching Dime the snow-plough and he's ready to go skiing for the day, so I could forget about him.

Phil, on the other hand, did not learn so well. In fact it was worse than that: I've never seen the guy so petrified in my life. It wasn't like the slopes we were going down were steep either; these were fucking bunny hills, and here's Philip H. Anselmo—one of the most confident, intimidating singers in metal even at that time—shaking like a leaf with fear. In this situation he wasn't such a tough guy after all.

Dime's brother's approach was different still: he was a fucking menace to society. His fat form dressed in a ridiculous parka jacket, I'd catch sight of Vinnie out of the corner of my eye, and he'd almost always be ploughing through gates, trees, families, leaving all kinds of destruction in his wake. It was like a cartoon and he had no idea how to stop. Vinnie Paul on skis was a man out of control, and more worryingly still, he seemed to have acquired a taste for this kind of action.

"Turn, you fucking idiot!!" I would yell at him, as he headed straight toward and flattened yet another innocent family without so much as an apology. Instead Vinnie just hauled himself to his feet and tried to get his skis back on again, but hadn't figured out how hard that was when they're pointing directly down the mountain.

... *Crash!*

He's on his fat ass again.

The experience was killing me. I wanted to leave, or better still, go get a drink. It seemed the only way to relieve the stress of Vinnie's constant collisions. So, halfway through the day we decided to get to the other side of the mountain where the bar was, but this involved hauling ass cross-country style and using T-bars to get uphill. You stand there and they pull your ass up the mountain. Sounds easy, but guess what? This was an idea that Vince just could not grasp and he spent most of the time rolling on the ground like a beached whale, right where people were trying to go up the hill.

Not happy with simply lying there, he's actually trying to grab ahold of other people as they go past him as if to say: "Hell, if I'm not going up, I'm going to make damn sure you aren't either." Vinnie just couldn't get the idea that these lifts do everything for you.

"See you later, fat boy!" we'd shout as we left him behind, trailing in our wake, pissing him off like hell.

Finally we get to the top and get a beer, and fat boy eventually joins us for the last run of the day, for which Vinnie had clearly held back his pièce de résistance.

After drinking a few beers and shots, I ski down, which was the first proper ski run I'd had all day due to having to look after these guys, and suddenly I see Vinnie speeding down toward another group of people.

I think: Where's he going? … He's not stopping.

Beyond the group of people, in Vinnie's immediate flight path, is a fucking huge, orange sign that warned skiers about the imminent danger of skiing off the edge of this huge, fucking mountain. He's like a giant Texan snowball, and he's gathering alarming speed, As always, something got in the way, and after crushing another family, this fat fuck slams into a hospitality tent full of people. They weren't amused. Vinnie didn't care.

"Fuck you, Rex, skiing is bullshit. I won't be doing this again, no Jack," Philip said as he carried his skis down the hill, swearing that he would never be back. He was white as a sheet. He didn't know how to stop and didn't know how to slow down, so it turned out that "Mr. Unscarred," as he called himself, was the biggest pussy on the hill and he would never, ever put on a pair of skis after that. This was a perfect example of how much of a contradiction Philip can be.

CHAPTER 9

DANGEROUSLY VULGAR

Touring *Cowboys* lasted almost two years, although because it was all so new to us, it seemed like no time at all. We had very few days off, not even to do laundry, and the only real gap came in the summer of 1991, prior to an important phone call from Mark Ross.

He asked us if we wanted to go to Moscow to play a concert, which was going to be recorded for a video, and of course we said, "Yeah." Because we had gotten so used to rejection in the past we said "Yeah" to most opportunities now and this one seemed a good one, although we didn't know too much about where we were going other than that Russia was famous for vodka. But before traveling overseas, we went back into Pantego Sound with Terry to lay down drum tracks for what would be our next record. This was a very critical point in the evolution of music, particularly the kind of music we were playing, and things were definitely about to change in the coming months and year.

Nirvana and the whole grunge movement hadn't quite taken over, but we'd heard the demo tapes for *Nevermind* because we'd had them played to us by Dale Kroeger from the band the Melvins. We all thought Nirvana were fucking great and we also loved Soundgarden. Then, on the other hand, you had Metallica, who came out with something overtly commercial like "Enter Sandman," and while it didn't completely change heavy metal, it certainly gave us a little opportunity to seize hold of an opportune moment in time when we most needed it.

Meanwhile Mark told us to get our gear packed and ready to ship so that we could be flown over business class. When we arrived in Russia, a translator and a bus met us. Well, the first thing we all notice is that there's no neon light in Moscow—no signs or ads for anything—and the whole place is lit up by what looks like just sixty watt light bulbs.

WALTER O'BRIEN

Because the Russian federation had taken over only weeks previously, there was technically nobody to grant us visas or anything so we had to have letters from the mayor of Moscow, the President of Russia, and someone heavy in the army, explaining what this was so that when we got to the airport we had to convince them to let us in. It took a couple of hours of juggling and bribing this and that person to allow us into the country. It was pretty wild!

———

"What are all these people doing standing in line around the corner?" I asked the interpreter, seeing scenes I just didn't recognize.

She said they were waiting for a loaf of bread and we looked at her in disbelief. We'd never heard of shit like that happening, anywhere. Moscow had only just gotten its first fast food restaurants, so there were lines outside McDonald's and Pizza Hut because these people had simply never eaten fast food. This wasn't the post–World War II era or something, this was the fucking '90s!

WALTER O'BRIEN

What's the thing you see a lot of when you're driving around a major city? Restaurants, restaurants, and more restaurants. In Moscow there were no restaurants whatsoever. We did find what people referred to as "the one good restaurant in town" and when we got there it was like you were eating in somebody's living room. It was a buffet and everything on the menu was cabbage. Cabbage with this, cabbage with that, fried cabbage, boiled cabbage. Which was fine if you like cabbage but of course this was Pantera so they said, "We want brisket barbecue, goddamnit!" which they didn't have so we ended up living on McDonald's and Pizza Hut.

When we got down to the tourist areas, Gorky Park and Red Square, places like that, the initial impression of back-asswardness was further confirmed. There were a bunch of black market stalls selling cassette tapes of just terrible recording quality, but the people thought this was great, which it probably was compared to how things had been in the past.

So that explained why before coming over, we were advised to bring two things: extra toilet paper and Levis—anything we had with Levi on it—because we were told we could barter with that stuff to get better deals on almost anything simply because these things—good toilet paper and jeans—just didn't exist in Moscow.

WALTER O'BRIEN

The first thing I wanted to do was to go down to Red Square and see the place you've seen so often on television, but it was late at night when we got there. So we asked our translator if we could go, and they said, "It's possible to go tomorrow." In Russia that means "no." So Rex and I went into the subway station and found our way to Red Square, where we wandered around, and people were coming up to Rex—they knew who he was.

———

We stayed in the first American hotel they ever had there, right across from the Embassy, and that was very strange also because it was not in any way luxurious. What must the shitty hotels have been like?

WALTER O'BRIEN

All the bands were booked in the Moscow Radisson, which wasn't even due to officially open for another three weeks. And what happened was that there was a major state department meeting going on between the U.S. and Russia, and they were working out of the hotel, too. We went into a ballroom upstairs and it was set up with a hundred tables with a black phone and a red telephone on each one. The red phones were secure lines back to America. One time I was coming out of the elevator and Wolf Blitzer from CNN was walking out! There was a restaurant in the hotel which everyone recommended we ate at and it said on the board "Special Today: Meat and Vegetables," so Rex asked, "What kind of meat is it?" so the guy behind the counter shrugged his shoulders and said, "It's meat." Rex said, "But what *kind*? Beef? Pork? Veal? What is it?" and the guy again just said, "It's *meat*."

———

The next day they let us sleep in before they took us out to Tushino Airfield, which was the site for the concert. As we arrived, they were just starting to set the stage up and kids were already starting to camp amid a sea of old war planes, turret guns, and what looked like fucking space satellites, all of which were just laying out in a huge field. It was one of the most surreal sights I've ever seen.

Equally surreal probably—for the million or so fans that were reportedly there—was the line-up for the gig: A-list heavy metal and rock deities in fact. There was AC/DC, Metallica, us, and the Black Crowes, and all I can remember is this big fucking sea of people at this huge airfield and flags from every fucking country you could think of. Shows like this by Western musicians were previously unheard of in the Soviet Union (as it turns out the new Russian federation took over the country a couple of months after we left), so there was definitely the sense that for the audience we were a glimpse of the exciting future rather than the repressive past.

But even so, the backstage facilities were definitely from a bygone era. The dressing rooms were like fucking tents, just terrible, with only one little light bulb for light. There were no refreshments whatsoever, maybe just a basic case of water, so fortunately we'd brought over our own liquids, but none of that really mattered because the show itself was fucking unbelievable and one of the best pieces of publicity that could ever come our way, too.

Like I said, we had already started thinking about and laying down drums on the new tracks before we went to Russia, but the whole experience breathed new life into the process when we got back. This record was going to lay the hammer down hard, and be the heaviest statement of intent we could possibly come up with.

! ♯ ⊕ *

WHEN WE RETURNED from the Moscow gig, Metallica's new record, the so-called "Black Album," was all over the radio. We thought it sucked, of course—I mean we thought it was just terrible—we didn't get the commercial sound of it at all and this made us even more determined to make our new record even heavier than anything we'd attempted before. It would be entitled *Vulgar Display of Power.* Our power.

At this point in our trajectory, despite the relative success of *Cowboys from Hell,* we still considered ourselves to be fairly small scale—and we were in a way, certainly in comparison to what we'd later become. From a critical-acclaim standpoint, things had definitely changed, but our lives hadn't altered radically so we were still very hungry for fame and cash. We were still doing our own little headline shows while also supporting the bigger bands, but nothing huge was happening to boost our profile as fast as we wanted.

We wanted to explode.

Despite being signed to a big label, we still felt like we needed to silence a few doubters with whatever we released next. What helped a lot was that when Metallica dropped this big commercial record of theirs, they unwittingly gave us this big, fucking gaping hole in the market to fill. While we definitely did have firm ideas for how we wanted the record to sound, Metallica's record confirmed to us that we were the band to take over the void they'd just left behind.

So when we actually walked into the studio to write them, the songs were just jumping out of us. It all seemed just so easy and natural. Consequently the *Vulgar* material was very well rehearsed even before our producer Terry came down to record them, and like *Cowboys* previously, we already had the demos down really well. We had a couple of bits and pieces left over from *Cowboys* and they became the tracks "Regular People" for sure and parts of "Hollow" maybe, but the rest of the tracks were completely fresh material. "Piss" was another track that I partly wrote at the time, but because the rest of the record was so strong, it just didn't make the cut. We ended up using part of it on "Use My Third Arm," which would later appear on *Far Beyond Driven,* but in 2011, "Piss" was released as it was originally conceived, on the 20th anniversary edition of *Vulgar Display of Power,* and I'm very proud of my role in it.

It's hard to remember which track we started with, but once we got going it was just nonstop—with ideas flowing from us, and we increasingly realized that, with our grass-roots, heavy sound, we really were the band to fill the slot that Metallica had just vacated. We believed we had the right profile to occupy that position of theirs and it was our perseverance and sheer desire to make increasingly heavy music that allowed us to do that. It was all on our terms and nobody else's. It wasn't on Metallica's terms or anything like that, and there also wasn't a whole lot of competition at this particular point in the '90s, but I can't think of many bands in our genre that, instead of going out of our way to appeal to an audience, made an audience gravitate toward *us.* That's an important distinction to make, I think, because it's such a rare thing in this world of following trends and fashions.

"A New Level" and "Fucking Hostile" were key songs in the process, and the fact they were so easy to do meant that we didn't ever want that creative flow to stop. It didn't seem like working, either. This was just living life while at the same time doing what we wanted to do, under no pressure whatsoever other than what came from our own unstoppable inner drive. Sometimes we'd sit in the studio until four in the morning, just coming up with different ideas while at the same time working on improving our overall performance level, which as a result of almost two years of live shows, was already as tight as a motherfucker.

As well as being more honed collectively, things had evolved for the band on individual levels, too. Phil's vocal range was way broader than it had been on *Cowboys* and that definitely gave us more variation when it came to making the music heavier. He still had the ability to hit the high notes for sure, but because he was a little bit older, he was also developing a tougher voice that complemented what the rest of us were doing.

Every song started with a riff of Darrell's, or something that Vinnie had, a drumbeat or rhythm pattern, or an idea from me or Phil. In some cases the idea process could just be something as simple as us going outside, smoking one, and seeing what happened when we got back in. Usually something did happen.

I definitely remember that when we did "A New Level," there were all these weird chromatic chords that we hadn't even tried before, and as it took shape it was like opening a book about something that you are really into, or better still, opening a Christmas present that you never thought you'd get in a million years.

Every single track we recorded had that certain something about it in a way that only the most vital albums can boast, and we all knew how good this fucking record was. There would be times when we were in the studio, like when "Walk" was coming together, and we'd be jamming on it with insane tightness. We'd look at each other in amazement and say: "Oh my God, how the fuck did we do that?"

It might sound like a cliché, but there really was magic at work with what we were doing on *Vulgar*, and we never again played and got along as well as we did at this time. Dime and I deeply understood each other as far as the chording, changes, and rhythm were concerned, and that in itself was a fucking amazing feeling, to be totally locked-in with your musical partner. Of course, Dime always knew *exactly* what he wanted to hear. He had that down to a tee. But sometimes I'd hear something from a bass player's perspective and would go in and put in my two cents worth. When he was doing leads, my role was to figure a bass line that fit.

On *Vulgar*, the demand for total sonic perfection was what we were aiming at. We used to sit down together, turn everything off at the board except for all guitar channels and the bass channel, and listen to the tracks with immense concentration, pay attention to every detail. Sometimes I'd test my ability by playing along to the track, and sure enough I was always right on the money. That's how tight we were, and we started calling this process "The Microscope," and from that point forward, applied that level of scrutiny to everything we did. Yes, we were heavy and aggressive, but the finer details really mattered.

TERRY DATE

For the most part, the process for working on *Vulgar* was similar to *Cowboys*—except that *Cowboys* was a little more advanced when I came on board. With *Vulgar*, they had just come off a very successful tour and they had riffs figured out, they knew they wanted to get harder and more intense but the songwriting process was exactly the same: they were great at working in a very small garage studio. If you look at how music is recorded in bedrooms now, well, it wasn't that much different for us back then because they were so comfortable working in Pantego, which, while very nice, is very humble compared to a studio in L.A. It's not the equipment in the studio or the walls that matters, it's how comfortable the players are, and they were very, very comfortable.

———

Although all the songs on *Vulgar* were super-heavy, it wasn't heavy for the sake of it; they also had killer hooks. Listen to "Fucking Hostile" and you can hear that, despite how fast and heavy it is, it's still just classic, good songwriting.

Not everyone shared our excitement. I will always remember the old man, who by this time had no role other than owning the studio space, but still thought of himself as our unofficial manager, coming in and hearing Philip's distorted vocals on "Fucking Hostile" and saying in his usual super-negative way, "Son, boys, y'all can't put that on the record, nobody's going to listen to it!" He *hated* distortion.

"You can't do it that way," he would continue, and we just said, "Did you ever hear of Ministry, dude? Go fuck yourself, and leave us alone."

He was like that about most things. If Phil shaved his head or some stupid shit like that, he thought we needed a fucking band meeting to discuss it. He was just one of these guys who wanted to limit us with his stupid little hillbilly ways and so he would say things like: "That's not how country music was done, and you just can't do that." As if country music even fucking mattered to us!!!

We just said, "Fuck you, sure it can." And we did it and it worked. We wanted to change the world with the music we were doing and that record did that. It definitely changed the game for a lot of fucking people.

! # ⊕ *

BEFORE THE ALBUM was released, we went out on tour with Skid Row in January of 1992, went out there and slaughtered them every night. These guys had a pretty heavy record out, *Slave to the Grind*, and had just come off the road with Guns N' Roses in Europe, so this was their very first headlining tour, with the craziest stage set-up I've ever seen in my life, just stupid with all the ramps and shit.

None of that concerned us. We just went out and did our thing night after night, and suddenly Phil had less of a "kill the world" vision and more of a "Look, here's an opportunity of a lifetime, we can steal *all* these motherfucking fans" type of mentality. He was very much more congenial on that tour, and we were really having a good time, taking names and shit. We also had the chance to let people hear the mastered tapes of *Vulgar* while we were still waiting for the artwork prior to the release date a month or so after the tour began.

We were travelling in our first full-blown tour bus and we thought, "Wow, so this is what we're going to be travelling in?" It seemed big time. We got our own bunk, which was a big step up from the motor homes we'd been out in the past, and there was also a driver so we didn't have to drive anymore, although we sometimes did, just for fun. One time we were going through Canada and it was me and Dime in the front seats. We went through the border control and they said to Dime, "What citizenship are you, sir?"

"Regular, sir," Dime said.

Dime wasn't the most intelligent of guys, at least in an academic sense, although he did have his different ways of trying to appear that he was. I'd call him Socrates sometimes to piss him off because he'd come up with what he thought was a brilliant idea, but to everyone else it was so fucking stupid. He'd use these big words, and I'd just say "Yeah, okay, Socrates Plato." But what he lacked in pure academia, he more than made up for in street smarts.

GUY SYKES

The tour with Skid Row broke Pantera in America, period—end of story. Heavy music in general was moving in different directions: you were either with Nirvana or Soundgarden in that genre, or you were moving harder toward Slayer and Metallica, and Skid Row was trying to move away from their hair band roots. On the Priest tour nobody had known what to expect: they got spit on, had shit thrown at them, and sold two or three t-shirts a night, but when we got on the Skid Row tour everything clicked. Pantera went out and destroyed Skid Row nightly, and that's what launched them to the next level.

———

When we played the new *Vulgar* material on the road it just blew everybody's fucking mind. Nobody said, "Oh well, that's nice" or something equally noncommittal; jaws were dropping, and though we didn't need that confirmation, we knew we were on to something huge.

Darrell had given us this really, really bad eighth-generation picture of a guy getting his face punched—all distorted like a bad photocopy. The label went and got a model with somebody punching him at a photo shoot and got the whole thing done up really nice, while also copying the spirit of what Dime had brought. Well, he got furious because he wanted to use the bad photocopy as the cover! We tried to explain to him that it couldn't be done. He actually wanted to use the original picture he had for the album cover!

———

Of course we were right about *Vulgar* and the record debuted at number forty-four on the album charts, which was completely amazing, and from that point on all of our friends and peers in other bands were coming out and trying to equal or better what we had done. The competition was on.

Jerry Cantrell was a good friend by this time, and it soon became a competition between me and him to be the first to have a certified Gold album. Alice in Chains were always just that one step ahead of us though, and they had hit the fuckin' jackpot with *Facelift* already, and would do even better with their next record later in '92. I was like, fuck, here we are sitting on 300,000 sales—and that's not bad—but Jerry had a Gold record and I was pissed!

While *Vulgar* wouldn't be our best-selling record in unit sales, it was our most significant because of the era in which it arrived. Heavy metal was changing because of the whole grunge thing, so most metal bands either had to change their sound to fit the trend or risk being forced back underground and return to the club scene. Pantera was the exception in that we actually thrived in these seemingly barren times for metal, and while playing heavier music than most people had ever heard before.

Despite our high profile and all the possibilities that were out there for us, fame and fortune would still be slow to arrive. *Vulgar* definitely got us on the ladder to stardom and to playing larger venues, so to return the favor that senior bands had shown us on our way up, we took out emerging bands with us on our headline tour—guys like Sepultura and Fear Factory who were trying to get their own thing going. Yeah, we now had the clout to sell out amphitheater-sized places, but we always respected where we came from and that was always one of Pantera's best qualities.

As far as our buddies in Metallica were concerned, well we hardly ever saw them after this point. On the rare occasions we did, Lars would turn up backstage with fucking dudes like John McEnroe. It was crazy shit. They seemed to be going down their own weird path anyway, and by the time they released *Load* in 1996, and had cut their hair and were wearing makeup, Pantera were headlining fucking arenas all over the world, never hanging out with the so-called cool people—I don't think our music was ever accessible enough to attract that kind of celebrity crowd, and I never had any big, famous people in my phone book.

Unlike Metallica, we didn't have the hit records on the radio that were the likely draw for celebrity hangers-on. But we *did* always have loyal, die-hard fans—sweaty teenage kids—that could sell out arenas every fucking night of the week.

On the other hand, all the musicians would come to our shows because they knew it was likely to be a huge party. If there was a Pantera show in their town, they knew they had to come out, show up, and by God it was going to be full on. Crazy shit would happen and it was fun.

The Metallica connection was kept alive briefly when we went out with Megadeth as openers on their *Countdown to Extinction* tour. The only emotion I can attach to the experience is that they were bland to hang out with. Our bands were polar opposites. We were in our heyday of getting fucking wasted every night, whereas they were on their whole sobriety kick, so the two don't exactly fit together. Dave

Mustaine would sneak in bottles of Scope mouthwash or shit like that to drink, which seemed so dumb to me at the time. I felt like saying, "Just go down to the liquor store, dude, and get yourself a fucking bottle of something. Fuck it, don't be drinking Scope!"

THE SUCCESSFUL TOUR had a sting in the tail for me personally though. My mother Ann had been in a wheelchair for a long time, since her muscle condition had gone sour. One day she was trying to reach for a bottle of Dewar's with a grab-handle, and she had an aneurism—fell out of the wheelchair and passed away immediately. I believe I was in Ohio somewhere and my sister and I knew that it was coming. We cancelled five days worth of shows and within a week I was back in Dallas putting my mother to rest. RIP Mom.

I had lost both my parents by the age of twenty-nine. But for me with my mom's passing there was a sense of relief. Her body had just given out. She'd had private care for a year and a half, Medicaid was running out, and it was starting to cost my sister and I a lot of money. I wish she were still here now to see her grandkids, but she's not and in the end her passing brought mixed emotions. On one hand it was a blessing and she was at peace, but at the same time I had lost my mother.

Ironically, the day after I put her in the ground, she got a Gold record for *Cowboys from Hell* in the mail. The same woman that told me that if I didn't study at school I was going to be a ditch digger. She definitely would have been very proud of her son, though, and in any case, once we got popular she learned to respect that I had in fact made the right decision when I decided to pursue music.

EVEN WITH A SUCCESSFUL TOUR for *Vulgar*, visiting places like Japan and having other life-changing experiences, I was still living in an apartment with John 'The Kat' Brooks, our drum tech, in North Arlington, a twenty-minute drive from the studio. That was the only part of town that I liked.

It was around this time I met my future wife Belinda through mutual friends who set us up. She wasn't into the music scene and didn't actually know who I was, other than I was in a band and had to play gigs. So in order to close the deal I bought a dachshund and said to her, "We still have to play gigs and someone's gotta take care of this dog while I'm gone, so you might as well move in." Which she did. I suckered her in with a wiener dog. So we moved into a high-dollar apartment in a gated community, and it was a real nice place to be.

CHAPTER 10

CONTROLLED CHAOS

We were on a break during late spring and the summer of 1993—God knows we had earned one—before we went into the studio to record *Far Beyond Driven*, which we started sometime in the fall of that year.

Things were a little different this time around because the old man had moved his studio up north to Nashville, built a place called Abtrax Sound, and the boys just couldn't get enough of giving their old man money—so we all went up there, too.

He had moved up there to get some of the country music market that he couldn't get down in Arlington. Also, because he had part of the publishing rights for *Cowboys* and *Vulgar*, *he* was getting paid what we were getting paid. (I'll come back to what I did about all this later.)

TERRY DATE

In the past there were pieces of tracks that everyone would work on and then come together and listen to, but with *Far Beyond Driven* everyone was there all of the time and there were certain advantages and disadvantages with that.
That's the best way of putting it. It was a completely different vibe.

———

So, we'd go up there for two weeks, three weeks max, and stay at the Holiday Inn in town. This was the beginning of Vinnie Paul's infamous strip club days. Of course at that time we'd all go in there and have a good time; it was a "bring your own beer" kind of deal, but he really got an unhealthy taste for it, and you'll see how that plays out later.

The routine became well tested: we'd work for a while, take a week off and go back to Texas, and write all this material, which, like on *Vulgar*, was just pouring out of us. Dime and Phil were both on fire creatively, and the opportunities were increasing because everyone could see how big Pantera were getting. We were asked to put a song on a Black Sabbath tribute record called *Nativity in Black,* so we did a cover of "Planet Caravan" on which I played fretless bass and keyboards. Unfortunately, we couldn't get the rights organized, which is typical of how labels don't want to give their band up, so it would become a bonus track on *Far Beyond Driven.* Good to know you're being protected, I guess, but frustrating sometimes, too, when you want a song on a high profile record.

One day we were sitting in the studio, baffled by Vinnie, who had this one weird drumbeat he was working on. Then, for some reason Dime plugged in one of these new whammy pedals that Digitech had just come out with, the kind that allowed you to change the octave every time you moved your foot. And that's how the songs "Becoming" and "Good Friends and a Bottle of Pills" came about—through simple, unscheduled experimentation.

I had used mostly Charvel basses up until this time, but I'd just gotten a deal with Music Man and was using their StingRay bass because I was really looking for a change. I knew the bass sound I wanted—a tone that would really pop out in the mix—but I just hadn't found it yet. I had all these guitar companies sending me coffee table–looking guitars; basses like Warwicks would come in and I'd plug them in and they sounded like crap. I eventually called my buddy Rachel Bolan from Skid Row and said, "Hey man, can I borrow a couple of your Spectors? I really want to check out and see what those things sound like."

I tried them on a couple of songs like "5 Minutes Alone" and after that I was a full-blown Spector fan. I had to have one and I've played them ever since. They cut through the mix a lot better. I'd always been a fan of Eddie Jackson from Queensrÿche, who also used them on their early records where you could really feel a bass punch come through. I really liked the tone that he had, but at the same time I was also trying to get some of my mentor dUg Pinnick's sound, too. dUg 's band Kings X were very influential for some of the more melodic material that Pantera wrote. It's not easy to identify, but it is definitely in there. He's also a big fan of us as a band and he was always on the sidelines cheering us along.

You have to remember that metal records don't always show bass sounds in their best light. Obviously I was a huge admirer of players like Geezer Butler and John Paul Jones. In purely metal terms, I really didn't like the sound that, say, Jason Newsted had in Metallica. To me it was just a bit "Ughhh." Just not my kind of bass tone at all. Someone like Gene Simmons always sounded really bland to me, too, and then at the other end of the spectrum you've got someone like Lemmy. Lemmy is just *Lemmy*. He's one of his own, and while you can say you're influenced by him, you'll never ever get that tone.

Working on *Far Beyond Driven* I also decided I really wanted to try out a five-string bass so *Music Man* sent one over (this set a precedent for equipment) and I loved it immediately. Not only did it sound good, it also allowed me to go down a fifth and hit the lower octaves that just aren't accessible on a regular four-string bass. This added totally different dimensions to the songs, almost like playing a new instrument, so maybe there was something motivating about playing one.

What we were all doing was experimental to some degree, but we also had these insanely catchy riffs to back it all up, like the ones that became "I'm Broken" and "5 Minutes Alone," riffs that we would come back to and refresh after we'd lived with them for a couple of weeks of driving around Nashville in a rental car.

The first song we actually wrote for the record was "25 Years," and I remember it mainly because Phil had these really fucked up lyrics that he was working on at the time about his father. When I first heard the horrible sentiments in there I said to him, "Dude, you just can't put those lyrics down there, that's your father you're talking about." To me it just wasn't cool, but you couldn't tell that dude what to do or not do, ever.

Three-quarters of the way through the process, we took everything out of Abtrax and moved the whole process to Dallas Sound Lab, which turned into a party every single night. By now Vinnie was heavily into taking ecstasy. It was just brutal watching him. I'd done it way back in the day when it was legal and good, not cut with speed and shit, but the stuff that was available in '93 made you wake up the next morning with your back totally spazzing out.

Also, when Dime and I did it back in the old days, we were smarter about how we took it. We'd just break little *chips* off the pill, instead of taking a whole one all at once that knocks you sideways, because that way it's easier to control the buzz. Vinnie took whole pills and the results weren't pretty.

All my bass parts were pretty much done in Nashville, but the rest of the guys were doing various overdubs while Phil came in to finish some of his vocal refinements, although he was pretty much done, too, as I recall. So on the occasions when I showed up in the studio, there was basically just a party happening.

I'd say, "Well, this is nice. This is a fifteen-hundred-dollar-per-day lockout and you guys are sitting around playing pool and not doing fucking anything." I was irritated that everything was taking so long.

TERRY DATE

There were friends around in the studio, I do remember that. I also recall having a hard time getting people focused and into the control room to record because it seemed like there were a lot of distractions. But there were *always* a lot of people around these guys, and maybe because I keep my head down and focus on the job in hand, I missed a lot of what was going on. A lot of Dime's guitar parts were done at that time for sure and that was memorable. There was occasional talk of label issues but I had to eliminate all that kind of stuff and make sure that none of it affected the actual making of the record. I was just there to get from A to point B.

_____

Basically we spent around $750,000 on that record—renegotiated the contracts with East/West record label and the whole bit—and by God we used every single penny of that, a lot of it on a bunch of bullshit, including paying for a bunch of hangers-on to party on our tab. It seemed like everyone came out of the woodwork when we went back to Dallas, and most of them seemed to forget that we had a fucking record to make, and that applied to Vinnie Paul, too. Progress was slow, and if I was frustrated by the delays, Terry Date was pulling his fuckin' hair out a lot of the time.

We had no A&R guy but we did have a guy affiliated to the label called Derek Oliver, but he wouldn't even show up. He knew fuckin' better. The room would have just told him to go fuck himself anyway.

The bottom line was that management left us alone because they knew we were putting out hit records—selling ten thousand units a week—so they knew not to fuck with the formula by interfering in the studio.

! # ⊕ *

TOWARD THE END OF 1993, during the process of finishing *Far Beyond Driven*, we headed to South America for the first time and that sure was a fuckin' trip. We flew all the way down to Buenos Aires and our first impression was that it was home to the most beautiful women on the planet, although we literally couldn't get out of the hotel to see them because there always seemed to be five hundred kids sitting outside, day and night, amid tight security.

I wanted to go and see the city and on days off Vinnie and I would always go and play golf, so we needed security to take us where we needed to go. We deployed a decoy system. We had two minibuses: one would go this way and the other would go that way and everyone would usually follow the first bus not knowing that we'd taken another route in the second to go and play this little golf course. This place was unique because it had caddies—none of whom spoke English—and we had to walk the course, something we never did at golf courses back home.

We'd say, "Gimme a seven iron!" and the caddy dude would run over to us with a fucking two iron or something. "No, señor! I said a seven iron," we'd say—a two iron is fucking hard to hit with anyway—but they'd still always try to tell us what to do, those caddies. This was our way of getting away from all the bullshit and back in those days it was usually me, Vinnie, and Sykes playing golf for fucking tons of money.

Phil and Dime weren't really into that kind of thing. While we were on the links, they probably sat and got drunk in a bar, although Phil always liked to work out. Yeah, that was his deal. Dime, on the other hand, had a routine that was all his own. He would basically get up around 5 p.m., get something to eat, and then the party would start rolling all over again, every single day. So by the time we got back from the golf course, he had our shots already waiting.

The shows down there were crazy because they totally oversold them. There were no safety regulations, no fire codes, no nothing. We finished one show on that trip and went back to the dressing room for a while, as usual, and then we came back out while the crew was loading up, we saw these people sweeping where the audience had been.

There were a growing number of odd piles, five feet high all around, so we asked, "What the fuck is that?" There were so many kids there that it turned out these piles were black hair that they'd pulled out of each other's heads during our show. They were packed in there so tight they were just ripping each other's hair out! Crazy shit.

CHAPTER 11

YOU FAT BASTARD!

Not long before *Far Beyond Driven*'s release there was an issue with the cover art because, of course, we couldn't put a picture of some chick with a big steel fuckin' drill up her ass, you know? That was the original plan. Although the art department had brought the idea to us and we were all into it, for commercial reasons we had to sell out a little and soften the tone somewhat. So we changed it so that the drill was going through this guy's head instead. That seemed to be okay. From the very beginning, Dime had pretty much taken charge of the art ideas for t-shirts, posters, and all that promotional stuff, so the rest of us did our best to keep out of it.

They—the record company—would send us all kinds of rough ideas and we'd look at one and say "okay," but to me, all that mattered was the music. I couldn't give a fuck less if the album had the

109

pope on the cover. All I thought was that as long as the cover had the band's name in the biggest letters that would fit on there, it didn't really matter what else was there, with the exception of a picture of some chick on a fucking stripper pole—which the brothers probably wanted. That I wasn't having.

WALTER O'BRIEN

It wasn't that Dime didn't have good ideas artistically— he did, but he didn't have the technological expertise to execute them. I'm not even sure if the image they wanted was even a chick! But it was a huge drill going up *someone's* ass. But I had to explain to the band that none of the major chains that were going to sell the record were going to let that picture slide. We could have made this band a lot more money if they had just followed efficiency and hadn't tried to reinvent the wheel every time they did something. I always wanted the band to have full creative control over everything or at least up until the point that it was going to get an X rating and not come out. Walmart and other big chains said they wouldn't carry the record if it had an "Explicit" sticker on the front, so we made an alternate version, which the band hated. I just said to them, "If you want to sell three hundred thousand copies and have explicit lyrics, that's okay. But you have to be accepting of the consequences that you're cutting your own record sales in half."

When *Far Beyond Driven* eventually was released in March of 1994, it went straight to number one on the *Billboard* chart, which was fucking unheard of for a record this heavy and for a band like us who'd hardly had any radio or video airplay. Ironically, MTV's *Head-*

banger's Ball documented our promotional signing trip where Warner Brothers gave us a Lear jet to hit twelve major cities in only five days to sign copies of the record for our fans.

WALTER O'BRIEN

Part of our job was to work with stores and record labels on marketing to the *Billboard* Chart and we knew that all the talk in the business that week was, "Which record was going to enter at number one? Was it Bonnie Raitt, Ace of Base, or was it the soundtrack for some rap movie?" It wasn't even on anybody's radar that Pantera's album could be anywhere near that, so I went into the label and suggested the Lear jet idea for doing signings because we knew that the key to blowing up the charts was to sell as many records as possible in that first few days. That's how it works. So when we were watching the numbers come in on the Tuesday following the signings, we said, "We might actually pull this off" and then when the numbers came in it was like the pope had died. I was getting phone calls from everybody saying, "Pantera has entered the charts at number one?!" And we just went crazy. These guys thought they were a platinum act like Van Halen even when they were still playing in the Texas clubs, so they had self belief, and you need that. But when the fame really arrived with the private jets and the rest, it affected Phil and Rex most. Phil didn't want to get in a private jet and he didn't want to be seen getting into a limo, but after he tasted it for a while, things changed.

———

GUY SYKES

Our in-stores weren't a thirty minute or one hour
appearance at your local Tower Records; some of these
were five and six hours, making sure that every single kid
was signed. At this point in their career Pantera was a
juggernaut, running on all four cylinders in every sense.

———

Touring *Far Beyond Driven* was going to be a huge deal, that much
was immediately clear. When you have a number one record, everything changes on every level and folks who weren't your friends before were going to want to be.

We were playing amphitheaters by then and playing in venues like
that is just a numbers game as long as the seats are sold out, which
ours always were. The real key is concessions, because that's how you
make your money, even on seemingly simple things like car parking.

We wanted every single kid that came to our show to also spend
ten bucks on a t-shirt because when that happens, that's when the
really big checks start flying in. Everyone is satisfied. There's no loser
in that whole deal. Everything was paid for and the machine just kept
building and building to the point where we were simply unstoppable. We felt we were indestructible and we destroyed a whole
bunch of shit along the way. We found new ways of fucking shit up
just for fun.

We were asked to join the Monsters of Rock bill and play a show
in June in the U.K. Now, the sense of humor over there is a lot different and you'd hear the crowd chant, "You fat bastard, you fast bastard! You fat bastard!" usually directed at someone who was
overweight. Well, I think *KERRANG!* magazine—probably the biggest
fucking metal magazine in Europe at the time—put a cartoon picture
of Vinnie Paul on the cover with that headline.

As you'd expect, Vinnie didn't care for it at all and said he didn't
want to work with *KERRANG!* anymore. I said, "Look, you have to

deal with this. I don't care if your ego is bruised or not; this is their way of saying that they love you." But Vinnie just couldn't take it that way. He wanted to fight with one of the magazine journalists, which was strange because Vinnie historically did not like confrontation. And in any case, in my mind, if there was anyone who needed to be confronted it was his father Jerry; but at this time neither he nor Dime would even talk to their father.

The publishing rights had been a simmering issue since the *Cowboys* days, but the brothers were too chickenshit to call their own father, so they left me, the so-called lawyer, to do the intermediary stuff. It was really sticky and took a year to sort out.

I remember being on tour in Germany, trying to deal with all this crap, and it ruined more than a few days of what should have been a good time. Our lawyers were David Codikow and Rosemary Carroll, and they had pretty much put Nirvana on the map. Every Christmas there would be a big screen TV on our doorstep, a gift from the lawyers. It was the least they could do for us. David and I were involved in the bulk of the negotiations over the rights with Jerry. I'd get off the phone with Vinnie and Dime's old man, phone David and say either "This is going nowhere," or "Okay, now we're making progress," but the whole thing continued to be frustrating and took a lot of effort on both our parts.

My whole argument to Jerry was, "If you didn't write these songs, why the fuck are you getting fucking paid for them?"

"Uh, because I signed the deal," he would say. That's just how Jerry was; he always took the psychological approach.

"Well, you're not our manager anymore and you don't write the songs," I told him.

I tried to explain further, "It's like Barry Bonds Senior throwing a ball to his son in the front yard, then wanting half of his fucking income."

He'd signed a management agreement and now he wanted it to run in perpetuity, to which I just said, "No dude, this isn't going to work. You might have two sons in this band but there are two other guys who will fight you to fucking death." I also felt like saying, "You know, your own boys don't even want to talk to you dude, how does *that* make you feel?"

Yes, as I've said I had some music business knowledge, but because I was the only one who did I was stuck in the middle of it all because the brothers wouldn't deal with their father, and Phil didn't have a clue about any of this kind of crap. After it was finally settled, the brothers didn't talk to their father for many years. Dime eventually said, "Uh, I better get in touch with the old man," probably around the time their mother got sick.

WALTER O'BRIEN

The money started coming in from *Cowboys* around '94, so that's what triggered Rex's dealings with the publishing rights. There's always a year or two delay before the cash really starts flowing, but when the contract with Jerry Abbott came in, we looked at it and none of the signatures on it were the band's. Their names were there but the signatures weren't theirs. The brothers didn't want to go into a lawsuit against their dad, so we ended up settling for a lot of money, but I didn't know what else we could do at that point. How do you tell guys to sue their father? I just thought it was really lame on so many levels. Rex really knew what he was doing, and we were always telling each other about the latest music industry books that were coming out, and he was right on top of that stuff.

———

WE HAD OUR TOURING ROUTINE pretty well set by this point—from a day-to-day perspective at least. We'd drive overnight, rarely stay in hotels, which made sense because once you're already comfortable in your bunk, why get up and get into some hotel that's going to cost you another four thousand dollars per night?

In the early days we could use the showers at certain venues, work it that way, and when we had a day off, maybe we'd stay in a Howard Johnson, but once we had the budget to really make things happen, then of course we'd stay in the occasional five-star place. But we didn't do Four Seasons–type deals. We preferred an accommodation that was a bit more homely.

We had a travel agent, Shelby Glick, who found us hotels with kitchens, so if we wanted to go to a market and then cook our own steak that night, we were able to do that. I would usually cook. In fact we carried some grills under the bus and we used to have im-promptu barbecues. We'd invite other bands over and the whole bit. I'd throw down just *huge* pieces of meat so that there was enough for everyone.

So on the morning of the show—well, it wasn't really morning for us, I guess—we'd start moving off the bus at two or three in the afternoon. Dime and I were usually the last to get going. We'd go into these places two days before the show in many cases, and I'd spent time sitting there with the lighting guys, making sure we got everything set up right. Then we'd do a pre-production sound check the next day to make sure everything sounded exactly as we wanted it to through the huge PA.

From there all we needed to do was tell our tech, "Look, I need a little more this or less of that," but that obviously changed from venue to venue. Occasionally we would sound check, but only two times a week at the very most because we always pretty much knew what we were going to do in terms of sound.

I wouldn't do much practicing before shows, certainly not in the latter days, and any preparation I did do would be centered on getting used to the weight of the instrument and doing all kinds of stretches. There would be a whole lot of water drinking going on and then, as I said before, a whole lot of booze going on after the water drinking.

Then, after the show the proper party started. Sometimes I just wanted to smoke weed, but the problem with weed is that it really fucks with your whiskey drinking. The quality and strength of weed has really intensified over the years since we started. Nowadays I can't even smoke that hydroponic shit. I hardly ever partake if at all. But if I wanted to smoke back then, I'd just go back to the bus because I hate being around people when I was basically paralyzed.

We'd also eat dinner on the bus, and for me that was usually an entire tray full of vegetables, the kind you can get at the market, because I always wanted to keep my slim figure. Food was always an issue with all of us. We knew what we liked and we stuck with that, and regardless of how well-travelled we were becoming and how many opportunities we had to dine like kings, we always gravitated toward what we knew, sometimes regardless of cost.

WALTER O'BRIEN

They were never exactly what you'd call world travelers. They'd go to France and say, "Why don't y'all have hot sauce over here?" They'd go to Germany and want spaghetti and get pissed off when they couldn't get it. At one point Vinnie insisted that they wanted lemon pepper on their food over in Europe and the catering company only had citrus pepper. It's the same spice, everything was the same, except it didn't say "Lemon Pepper" on the bottle. So they ended up going behind my back and having one of the girlfriends ship a case of a hundred and forty-four bottles of lemon pepper overnight from Texas. And by the way, we ended up having to ship back a case minus two bottles at the end of the tour. They had no idea how to conserve money. I had it worked out that a tour to Europe could potentially make them $400,000, but when we got back it transpired that because of all the spending they had lost $200,000. They bitched at me, of course, that they were in the hole. "How could we have lost $200,000?" and I said, "You didn't, you actually lost $600,000" They didn't get it at all.

————

Being on the road was a war of attrition in every sense, and boredom was the enemy. There's just nothing to do when you're just sitting on the bus for fifteen hours, so inevitably it always seemed a good idea to crack open a cold one.

We also came up with games to play, and because we were now earning good money, the stakes were increasingly high. The guys in Biohazard taught us this dice game called *C-Lo*. There were three dice, and the tale of the tape is that you throw out all three and there's a banker who calls a limit of, let's say, a two-hundred-dollar max.

So someone rolls the three dice until you get a "number"; a number is when two of the dice are the same, and whatever the other one is, that's your number—which then has to be beat. So if I throw a five out there, it's a pretty good chance that I'm going to win everybody's two hundred bucks that's sitting around in the circle. We'd have pits of up to eight people at certain points so there was a lot of money changing hands at times. Because of the boredom on the road, we'd play this all the time. It was fun to do and everybody would sit around and drink beer and get some road camaraderie going. We'd get bus drivers, truck drivers—everybody would play. It could get ugly, too. When you've got a bunch of drunks gambling, you need rules, and everything had to be settled in cash on the night, just like guys on the street would do in the old days.

On one leg of the U.S. tour we had Type O Negative with us as support, and we partied with Peter Steele every fucking night. He was a gentle giant. He would come out and sing "Walk" with us every night, and he would physically pick me up sideways and put me up to the mic so I could sing into it. He was fucking hilarious. On that tour we started doing other crazy shit on the bus like sending a runner out for the biggest double-chocolate fudge cake he could find, and then we'd have bets on who could eat it in the fastest time, while Dime and I would pony up money. None of these big dudes, especially Big Val, our head of security, could resist trying to eat the cake—he was always trying. We'd watch him get about halfway through and he'd be turning green.

Even when we went out for dinner and he'd already had a full meal, I'd buy Big Val another one and say, "Okay, dude, see if you can eat all this for this amount of money." He was always up for a challenge, thought he was fucking Superman.

We'd do the same with hot sauce, see who could drink a whole bottle in fifteen seconds without throwing up. It was all just good-natured ways of trying to kill time on the road.

! # ☮ *

THE STAGES WE WERE PLAYING were probably forty feet wide by twenty deep, and Phil had a microphone cable that was fifty feet long, which allowed him to run from one side to the other. The security routine on tour was always the same: at five p.m. every show day, Big Val would sit down with his whole crew and say, "Look, this is the way it's going to go. If a kid's getting out of hand, don't man-handle him, just get him out of the way. But make sure he's safe." Some of these kids were rebellious as shit and there's just nothing anyone can do about it; Val understood that but he wanted the hired security crews at the venues to understand it, too. It seemed that some of these kids in the '90s just wanted to go to a show to get their aggression out, and looking back on it now it was a hell of a lot of fun to instigate that kind of reaction. I'd much rather they did it there than on the street, that's for sure.

WALTER O'BRIEN

Phil had this bad habit wherever we played of saying to the crowd, "Our stage is your stage"—kind of like Jim Morrison in the '60s: controlled chaos—at which point there would be a near riot. He just wouldn't get the hint that if someone got hurt, they were going to sue him and that it was going to cost him more money than he makes, and it got to the point where there was no controlling him. So thereafter, anytime I was backstage at a show and heard it go quiet onstage, my first thought was, "Oh, no, here comes a lawsuit."

———

So during the show one night while we're playing some open field in Buffalo, New York, this big, steroid freak, one of the security crew, decides to manhandle some poor kid who's trying to climb the barrier that's ten feet from the stage. He pushed him to the ground, face down in the concrete with his hands behind his back. Then he picks the guy up by his fucking hair and starts pushing him along, by which time Phil has seen what's going on and is seriously pissed. So Phil—who can throw a fucking football like Drew Brees—launched his microphone and hit the security dude right on the back of the head and he fell to the ground. Suddenly, the promoter calls the show off and they lock-down the whole backstage area so there was no way we could get out. Phil then gets thrown in jail and the whole bit.

We all said to the police, "Wait, aren't you missing the point here?" but of course Phil got the blame and it cost five thousand dollars worth of bail, all for standing up for a fan who was getting beat up. It was fucking crazy. This kind of shit wasn't new either. It got to the point where I saw incidents from onstage and I just wanted to take off my fuckin' bass and sling it. I felt like saying to these clowns, "These kids came to see us, not you, cocksucker." It's not like these security guys own these places; they get paid fuckin' six dollars an hour to run security and then think it's okay drive one of my fans in the dirt because he's trying to jump the barricade. It was so stupid and something we just would not tolerate.

Phil usually controlled the crowd very well, but we had to stop our shows sometimes *because* of the security guys, not because of our fans. The upshot of it all was that Phil ended up having to go to court a year later after the trial was delayed three times, where he apologized (and pleaded guilty to an assault charge), got a fine, and was told to do a number of community service hours.

WALTER O'BRIEN

Management was on eggshells a lot of the time regarding what Phil was likely to do. We'd already had an incident on the *Vulgar* tour where I had to pay a guy off who was just looking for a quick buck lawsuit because he claimed Phil had assaulted him at a show in San Diego. In the end I paid him the five hundred dollars he asked for to settle even though we were ready to pay him *fifty* grand if we had to. He then told me that all he really wanted was five minutes alone with Mr. Anselmo, to which I said, "Trust me, you wouldn't *survive* five minutes." He'd then claimed that we were racists—despite later making racial references about me—so, when he'd been paid off by me personally with a cashier's check, I couldn't resist saying to him, "Not only are you a racist but you are also a fucking moron. I was prepared to pay you fifty grand to *not* go to court."

Whether the incident at that the Buffalo show was in any way symptomatic of Phil's spiraling frame of mind is hard to say. At this point in our ascendancy—approaching the highest point of our popularity as the biggest metal band of the decade—Phil's relationship with the rest of the band was slowly but surely starting to become distanced. Not breaking down, not yet, but there was a palpable separation that I certainly noticed. He didn't travel with the rest of us; he was on another bus with his assistant and his trainer who he always took on the road, so that diluted the unity we'd had on previous tours. Not just that, he was spending more and more time back home in New Orleans when he wasn't either touring or in the studio.

TERRY GLAZE

I was in Los Angeles and Darrell called me and asked if I wanted to come and see them play at some outdoor amphitheater type place and I remember being just stunned at how powerful they were. I mean, we were pretty tight when I was in the band, but this was something different. It was almost frightening. I've never seen a crowd like it: everyone bought a t-shirt and everyone sang along to every song. I don't know many bands that have fans that dedicated. I'll never forget that Dime took a shit in a bucket while he was playing onstage. Actually squatted down, pulled down his shorts and took a shit. They tried to bill him for the cleaning but he insisted that if they did, he got to keep the bucket. In his eyes, the bucket was *his*.

After the show they asked me onto the bus to travel with them to Reno, Nevada, and that was when I met Phil for the first time. He came up to me with a big smile and whispered in my ear, "I totally know why you bailed on these guys." That surprised me, but at the same time I felt that he and I were the only two guys in the club. We *knew* what being in Pantera was all about, but he felt confident talking to me because he knew he was in control. He had found his place.

———

There's no suggestion that his retreat was anything other than a reaction to fame or a simple need for privacy at this point but, looking back now, I suspect that this may have been the beginning of Phil's drug problems. We all knew he was having a lot of back pain, but even though we continually told him to go and get it checked out by a specialist, it was a long time before he actually did.

I finally said to him, "I'm tired of hearing about your back shit, dude, why don't you go to a doctor? We've got one right here in town, so why not go and get an MRI and see what's going on with it?" But for a long time he didn't do anything. "If you had a fucking cold every day for six months, wouldn't you think something was wrong?" I asked him.

When he eventually sought medical advice he was told that the recovery period for back surgery could be more than a year—time off that he couldn't tolerate—so he continued down the path of alcohol and other forms of pain relief to get him through the shows on the last leg of the U.S tour, which we did with Prong as our support.

But all that time Phil was always saying, "Oh, my back this, my back that." Because of the rampant painkiller culture he came from, down in New Orleans, he used to take Somas—muscle relaxers—to relieve the pain. But we all know that people gravitate toward a heavier drug if they can't get high off whatever they're using at the time, and in his case ten of these Soma fuckers just wasn't doing it for him.

WHEN WE WENT OUT on tour, we didn't do little four-week trips; we'd be out there for a year or more. So when we eventually finished touring *Far Beyond Driven* in late 1995, we had a few months off back home in Texas, and during that time Dime and Rita bought a house out in Dalworthington Gardens. It was a traditional, family home, the kind you'd find in somewhere like Savannah, Georgia, but it was located in the worst place you could possibly buy a house, in my opinion.

First, it was way out in the sticks in the southern suburbs of Arlington, which was a pain in the ass for me, and second there were more fuckin' cops per capita than they had people. As far as I was concerned it was not a safe place for a rock and roller to be.

But it did come with a huge, ready-built RV barn. This place was so huge you could have parked two buses in it. So Dime decided to use the space to build a home studio by constructing walls within walls so that the thing was completely soundproofed and wouldn't fuck the neighbors up or contravene city codes. Of course, he didn't do it himself—the builders did all that—but most of the organizing was done by the brothers, as it was, after all, Dime's home.

RITA HANEY

I had my own place in town—bought it two years previously—and when Darrell came off the road he'd come straight to my place where we'd grill and hang out by the pool and that really got him thinking about having his own place. Darrell wanted somewhere he could write and he only had this tiny four-track room at his mom's, which he'd finally outgrown. Dalworthington Gardens was the third house that we looked at, and I remember him looking at it saying, "Dude, this house is so big; I just don't think I can ever fill it up." Of course it took one tour of him coming home with all kinds of crap to fix that, so he bought it, and I transferred over there and sold my own place.

But what Darrell's new place meant for the band as a whole was that we now didn't have to book time anywhere to record, so in turn we basically took the money they guaranteed us for the next record—around eight hundred grand if I remember right—and spent it on that studio, from which I've yet to see any fuckin' cash, incidentally. It was a huge house, six thousand square feet at least, and a place where we could all convene, but it took a lot of building time to get the place fit to record a Pantera record.

TERRY DATE

Aaron Barnes, Vinnie, and I spent a lot of time making wires and putting the studio together. The band had an early version of digital recording gear at that time and they wanted to use it to record the album. I hated it. I talked them into buying an analogue tape deck, which we brought into the control room, set it up, and the thing was humming like crazy. We could not figure out why, we did everything we could, until finally we found out that there was fifty thousand watt power cable buried under the studio. So we moved the deck into the recording room where the band was but, when the band's recording, there tends to be a lot of Coors Lite going down and when something's empty those cans get thrown. They'd end up on the tape deck quite a lot so I had to build a barricade around the tape deck!

As I said, getting there was kind of a haul for me because I was still living in North Arlington. Vinnie still lived with his mom. In fact neither of the boys left their mom's house until they were thirty, but at least Darrell finally flew the nest.

I had just gotten married—in May of '95—so I was kind of focusing on something else, but I still had to work and my wife Belinda knew that. My focuses were, "Okay, let's get this shit done so I can go home. Let's not sit around and get fucked up all night long and not get anything accomplished," like we'd done on the last record when it took these guys six months to mix the goddamn thing. So while my head was elsewhere to some extent, I was still totally dedicated to the musical journey and where the next record, *The Great Southern Trendkill,* was taking us.

RITA HANEY

When Rex got married we were all kind of surprised. It was very quick. When Rex came off the road, he did a lot of things that Darrell and I had nothing in common with: we weren't golfers, weren't into the country club thing; we were still fans and into going out to dive rock bars and getting strapped up and that was something Rex never liked doing. We were in Hawaii when Rex proposed to Belinda. It happened on the beach and it was a fun night.

Being in a band and having a wife or girlfriend is a difficult balance for sure. I found an old calendar the other day, the kind you keep on your desk and write in the squares, and they were home in 1990 for thirty-eight days that entire year. I didn't get to see them a whole lot, but after *Vulgar,* when they got their own tour bus, that opened up a few more options as far as wives and girlfriends going on the road. The guys were really set on being that "Band of Brotherhood" and they wouldn't let relationships or chicks get in the way of that, so they were really careful how they structured that part of their lives. A lot of it was designated in that they would have something called "Chick Day" when all the girlfriends or wives would come out for that particular weekend so that everyone could be on their best behavior. I never really had to worry about that kind of thing with Darrell though because he was exactly the same whether he was in front of me or away from me; that's just how he was. I probably got to go out more often than others and didn't always have to go with the designated chick day. Everyone—including crew—went through a lot of women over time.

————

I can still remember the mental place I personally was in at the beginning of the writing process, and it really was a fucking cool feeling. Whenever I got off the road, I felt "I want to get as far away from you fucks as I can." It was nothing personal. These guys were my brothers, but I had a desperate need to keep my work and home lives as separate as humanly possible.

Hell, I'd rather go home and listen to fucking Frank Sinatra than go out and spend a thousand dollars a night just for the sake of trying to be noticed in town like others like to do. That just wasn't me at all and it never will be. I always needed the feeling of being grounded more than I had a desire to be seen. I had a totally different bunch of friends anyway and if we went out, we'd go out to the local hole in the wall bar rather than the clubs. I'd already played the fucking clubs for the early part of my career, so the last thing I wanted to do was hang out in them now. I had done all that shit, so why would I want to do it all again?

I craved stability because I had never really had it. I was moved around so much when I was young and spent so many nights as a teenager on somebody else's couch, it sometimes felt that my life was constructed on constantly shifting sand with no firm foundation. Now that I had the means and a solid relationship, I was desperate to address that feeling of insecurity.

I had this concept that I came up with about touring and the band, and I called it "The Light Switch." When I was on the road or in the studio, I was working—and the switch was "on." Then when I was at home and not working, the switch was "off," or at least it was *supposed* to be off. Turning the switch off was a challenge.

RITA HANEY

When Darrell wasn't with the band, he never saw the other guys. We all had totally different friends. Darrell would come home and totally detox—check in at the Rita Ford Clinic as he liked to call it. He didn't always want to get out. He'd sit and watch forensics on TV, eat food, and we'd just get fat. Get larded up as he'd say.

———

I was totally fed up with paying so much money on rent, so Belinda and I bought a new house in North Arlington, way up north, right down the street from where our apartment used to be, off Brown and Green Oaks.

It was a good, safe neighborhood on a big hill with a bunch of really nice but relatively modest homes, and I got this place for a fuckin' steal of a price. We were told that the whole area used to be owned by a Chinese guy who had a bunch of different stores in town, but he ended up torching his house while his family was in it, so they always said the place was kind of cursed.

I fixed up our place myself and enjoyed doing it, that's the kind of thing I *wanted* to do when I was home. Light switch "off" stuff, you know? I tore out all the carpets and put in wood floors. Then I put in Saltillo tile all the way through it and just made it my own home. When you walked out in the backyard it was all little bay palm trees with impeccable landscaping, gazebos, and the whole bit. I built a bar in the back with thousands of dollars of timber and it was domestic bliss. That place was killer!!!

Then a year later, Vinnie moved around the corner …

There was a piece of property up there at the top of the hill and

Vinnie liked it. Because he'd been living with his mom, I felt for sure that he'd just go somewhere down in South Arlington close to her. But instead he bought this huge piece of land that wasn't suitable for a home because of the pitch. But he liked the neighborhood. *My* neighborhood.

Remember, Vinnie didn't have any kind of style or sense of class, none whatsoever, so of course he built a house that looked like it should have been in Malibu, not Arlington, Texas. It looked fucking stupid, and to make things worse he also got really fucked over during the construction process. The project manager bailed on him halfway through the whole deal, and then the contractor also screwed him over bad. Worse still, he ended up having to put in thirty or forty thousand dollars of retaining walls because it was literally a ninety degree angle to get up to his house, so people used to roll their cars off the side of the hill just trying to get there. When I was bored I used to hit golf balls with a seven wood up toward his house, break a few windows and the whole bit, and if he'd been hitting back at me, he would have been hitting a nine iron down, so that should give you an idea of the elevation difference between our properties.

From then on I saw more of Vinnie, and having him around was like having the crazies move into the neighborhood. He was all gung-ho about it, too, he wanted this big party house, and so he had people over at his place every fucking night.

There was an incident at Vinnie's house when the Dallas Stars brought back the 1999 Stanley Cup. One of our songs became the PA intro to all the Stars home hockey games, and because Vinnie was a fan, he had become friendly with some of the players. Now, I wasn't there but I'm told that at first they all drank champagne out of the trophy. Then it went to Crown Royal, then vodka next, and then it went in the pool. It was a unique pool, too, because Vinnie appropriately had the Crown Royal logo tiled on the bottom.

Of course everybody knew where *my* house was, so they'd just throw beer bottles as they were driving past, shouting, "Huh huh, there's where Rex lives." If they'd hit one of my cars I would have gone up and made Vinnie pay for everything, that's for damn sure. My dumb mistake was that I got him a used golf cart one Christmas, painted it all camouflage with a fucking rebel flag and shit. He'd come screaming through my yard and knock sprinkler heads out, and that's when I said, "Umm no, I think it's time to go."

CHAPTER 12

GOING DEEP, HEAD FIRST

*T*he *Great Southern Trendkill*, from a musical sense, was all about further experimentation for us, and for a lot of our fans it's their favorite record. But personally speaking it's the record that was kind of lost on me. It's not commercial at all—I get that—but from a *band* perspective it had some fucking great music on it, but just not to my particular taste.

When we started it, we had an important collective decision to make: Where were we going to go? Here's a band that always says we're going to get heavier and heavier, but how heavy can you possibly go without the sound completely malfunctioning? The answer? Fucking heavier still.

Trendkill was done a bit more off the cuff than we'd tried before. We wrote in the studio, usually from a riff that Dime came up with, and instead of having, say, forty songs to choose from, we'd just focus on doing ten that were killer. Why spend your time on another thirty songs that aren't ever going to make it?

WALTER O'BRIEN

Phil kept wanting to go heavier and heavier and heavier, which was strange because he was just as likely to put on a Journey album on the tour bus as he was a Cannibal Corpse record. His big thing was saying how Metallica had sold out and he didn't mind going on stage saying that Metallica sucks and are a bunch of pussies. That was a problem when the other three guys in the band are asking me to get them on a Metallica tour!

Like before, Phil was in Texas for most of the writing process and we'd go in for two weeks until we became frustrated with one another and reached a point where we said, "All right, fuck it." And at that point Phil would fly out, home to New Orleans. We'd take a breather, maybe for a month, and then all get together again to start the process over, unlike the very early days when we went in for thirty days straight until it was done.

The daily routine went roughly like this: we'd get up, go and have lunch, and then start putting stuff together. When we'd come up with something we liked, we'd call Phil in to listen to it. He always kept nighttime hours. He'd then put in his two cents and we'd change things around until we found something we all liked. As always we were extremely precise about how things sounded. Sometimes I would keep my original bass track if I liked it, but eight times out of ten I'd fix the bass tracks later, which is difficult because you don't have that live feel you had when we were all playing on the floor.

I remember when we were doing the demos for some of the *Trendkill* tracks, and there was this bass thing that Vinnie didn't hear when it came to the final tracks. It totally threw him off course. I ended up redoing it because he picked up something he didn't quite understand—it was just a little piece of improvisation that I threw in at the last minute, but Vinnie said "No, you have to do it the way we did it on the demos." That's how rigid Vinnie was in the studio.

Despite any personal issues that Vinnie and I had or would have, we were always very synced in the studio. When we write, we pretty much go with the first idea that comes to us. We always relied on that gut instinct approach, so it would have been a mistake to start second guessing that because it had always worked to that point. Whatever drum lick Vinnie came up with, I just found a bass riff that went around it.

Not surprising, Terry Date claims he has six hundred hours of DAT tape from the *Trendkill* sessions alone, although I've never heard any of it.

Even as it stood, *Trendkill* was so difficult to play because we were playing lightning speed most of the time. This was thrash to the fucking ultimate. Metallica had taken loads of chances with what they were doing by releasing *Load*; when we were doing *Trendkill* we admired that, but I think it continued to push us in the totally opposite direction.

Personally, I like melodies over the top of heavy shit. That's important. You can't say that *Vulgar* didn't have hooks and *Far Beyond* didn't have hooks—they both did. But it was almost as if Phil went completely out of his mind with *Trendkill*, with his drastic vocal-and lyrical-style change. He'd also done the first Down record as a side project and done a few shows with them, too, and we all accepted that it was always going to be secondary to whatever Pantera was doing. Having said that, when I heard a few of the riffs off *Nola*, I said, "Oh my God, Phil, dude, save some of that shit." It was that good.

WALTER O'BRIEN

With the first Down record it was always accepted that it was a temporary thing. Phil had the tapes; he was playing around in the studio; they sounded great, so we said let's just put it out and do a short tour, then we'll all go back to Pantera.

———————

But it was obvious during the writing process that lyrically this record was headed down a much darker path, and if you're asking me whether that was connected to Phil's state of mind then I'd have to say probably so. The guy cut off all his fucking hair for one thing. I followed suit because my hair was down at my ass and I was just tired of it, but I think his reasons were altogether different. Not just that, he had started wearing wristbands and socks over his hands (presumably to hide something), so maybe his lyrics weren't the only indication of bad things to come.

I couldn't tell in his eyes that there was a drug problem, because I'd never been around anyone who'd been on heroin. But he would make these obvious gestures to me occasionally—hit his arm and shit like that, and I'd just say, "Really? You want me to join that club? Not interested, pal, and never will be." I knew pretty much what he was doing, but I don't think the other guys had any idea whatsoever. For the record, I never thought that alcohol and heroin would mix very well in my lifestyle. I thought it would have to be one or the other, and I chose alcohol.

RITA HANEY

I don't think anyone realized Phil's problem was as severe as it was, and I still believe to this day that back pain was an excuse to some extent, although I acknowledge the fact that he did eventually get back surgery. None of us wanted to see the problem, but in retrospect I look back and think, "God, how obvious was that?!" But, like all of us, I had never been around heroin so I didn't know what to look for, but there's no doubt that when Phil went back to New

Orleans, his friends used him as the dope supplier because he had money and he was isolated when he was down there. This wasn't the Phil that we knew, the "stronger than all," the "far beyond driven" guy, and I think we all wanted to ignore the fact that he'd changed.

———————

Phil *wanted* to be at home in New Orleans whenever possible—there's no doubting that. It seemed as if personal isolation went hand in hand with his drug issues, but he was still focused enough to deal with his vocal tracks as well as he ever did. What helped a lot was he had somewhere to do his work away from the rest of the band—Trent Reznor had a really cool studio that he'd just built down in New Orleans. Every time we stopped there we'd always go to Trent's place. We were hanging out pretty regularly—never toured together however—and Trent had made so much fucking cash from *Pretty Hate Machine* that he now had two different studios, both with SSL consoles, so there was sometimes a free console if Trent wasn't using both.

So it was always a case of "If you guys ever want to track down here, come on down." Phil took him up on the offer and Terry went down there to do the vocals, send them to us, and we'd either say "No" or just go along with the new direction Phil was heading in. Because we were apart, it made it difficult to have a conversation about the vocals, so to avoid wasting time, we'd occasionally say "okay" and move on.

TERRY DATE

Phil was becoming more distant. On the occasions I went down to New Orleans to do the vocals with Phil, I left my assistant in Texas with Pantera, and this was his first time with them to work on guitars. The first day I was gone, they put him down in a chair, super-glued his hair, dipped it in paint and then lit it on fire. That was his initiation. I took rough mixes of all the songs down and then we would just do one song every day. I'd go in mid-afternoon and Phil would come in on time every day with his lyric sheets written out, everything figured out with every line underlined that he wanted doubled. So it was really a quick process. I actually had him sing in the control room with me, standing twenty feet behind me with floor monitors and speakers in front of him. Then after a week or so I'd then bring everything back with me to Texas. and I'm sure there was some level of resistance because they wanted more singing and less screaming, that much I did know. There are always creative differences in any band.

———————

Maybe it was because he was out on a limb from the rest of us and in the initial grip of heroin addiction, but Phil's vocals sounded very different from any of the previous records. For a start he was doing a lot of double tracking and narration within songs. He would double-take one track, then come back with this other track, right behind it with these fast words, something that was almost impossible to replicate live. Then on the other hand he'd have an emotional, textured song like "Floods," which was simply beautiful. I remember when Dime first brought it to me; I fucking loved it immediately. Then I tried to come up with a bass line that worked and that swing style bass synced with Vinnie's drum pattern and became one of my favorite bass lines in our entire catalog.

RITA HANEY

The "Floods" guitar solo was something that Darrell used to play in the pre-Phil days, and he once made me a sleep tape, which I still have, consisting of ninety minutes of that solo, with all the harmonics, forwards and backwards, so

Six 8×10s, six 4×10s; the biggest selection of Ampegs ever! (Joe Giron Photography)

Samurai Rex! Somewhere in Japan.
(Joe Giron Photography)

Me and Dime before a show.
(Joe Giron Photography)

Photo session for *Power Metal*. Nice hair! (Joe Giron Photography)

Another day at the rodeo, touring *Reinventing the Steel*. (Joe Giron Photography)

Early days. (Joe Giron Photography)

Me and two jolly policemen,
Tushino Airfield 1991.
(Joe Giron Photography)

Onstage at Monsters of Rock,
Moscow 1991. (Joe Giron Photography)

Red Square, Moscow 1991.
(Joe Giron Photography)

The boys at Dime's studio recording *The Great Southern Trendkill.* (Joe Giron Photography)

Christmas in front of Dime's house
at Dalworthington Gardens.
(Joe Giron Photography)

Rio. (Joe Giron Photography)

Taking a breather during the set. (Joe Giron Photography)

Early days; Bronco Bowl, Dallas 1985. (Joe Giron Photography)

Saluting the fans, somewhere in America.
(Joe Giron Photography)

Me, Dime, and dUg Pinnick. (Joe Giron Photography)

Touring *Vulgar Display of Power* with the first Rex prototype *Fernandes* bass. (Joe Giron Photography)

Arcadia Theater, Dallas,
during *Power Metal* days.
(Joe Giron Photography)

Catching some surf; Gold Coast, Australia. (Joe Giron Photography)

In the studio circa *The Great Southern Trendkill* sessions. (Joe Giron Photography)

Me and my idol, Gene Simmons, in *RIP* magazine. (Joe Giron Photography)

Me jamming ballz-out ... somewhere. (Joe Giron Photography)

Having a good time in Dime's house. (Joe Giron Photography)

Touring *Far Beyond Driven*. (Joe Giron Photography)

At the Six Flags Over Texas amphitheater, 1985. (Joe Giron Photography)

Rex ... just Rex. (Joe Giron Photography)

One of the last of the good old days.
(Joe Giron Photography)

Touring *Vulgar Display of Power.* (Joe Giron Photography)

Somewhere in Europe. (Joe Giron Photography)

For my brother and friend, R.I.P. (Joe Giron Photography)

that I could fall asleep to it. But once I figured out Phil's lyrics and what they pertained to, I hated listening to it and it ruined the song for me. Obviously I got past that and I can now derive other things from the lyrics, but none of us realized that Phil had gone that dark and it was coming out in his lyrics.

————

CHAPTER 13

TRENDKILL OUT ON THE TILES

We started touring *Trendkill* after it came out in May of '96, and we were all hitting it extremely hard. When you're partying like that you really can't tell what the next guy's doing, so it wasn't as if we were watching Phil and wondering what he was getting into, because it was full-on debauchery for all of us in our own way.

The boys had built "The Clubhouse," a full-beaver strip club in Dallas with a loose, 19th hole golf-like theme. The place had all our records hanging on the wall and became a stopping point for almost every band that came through town. For Vinnie it was the culmination of his obsession—he now had his very own titty bar. I invested in it, too, and I'm glad I did because the return was three hundred percent. But apart from dealing with all the legal aspects in the planning process, I probably went in there only a handful of times. This was Vinnie and Dime's deal and not the kind of place in which I ever wanted to hang, though I'm happy to have made money from it.

Part of the reason they wanted the place was to entertain *their* friends. At home, they had a completely different set of people who wanted to be around them all the time. You can't criticize the brothers for it. That's what they did. You can't question what anyone's doing when they do what they want to do. They had this other family that I wanted no part of, and that was their choice. To a degree I would allow people to hang around me, even use me, but it got to a certain point where I'd rather knock somebody out than sit and listen to their bullshit. And I did many times.

We were playing a show in Dallas, one of the first shows on that tour, in July. It should have been a raucous homecoming but it turned into something else. I remember the night well, not because of anything particular other than there was something weird going on in Phil's dressing room, which was next door. I recall that all these crazy people showed up out of the woodwork and I just thought, "Well, this is kind of trippy." There was always weed being smoked in Phil's dressing room, heavily at times, so much that you'd get a contact buzz as soon as you walked in the door, but I wasn't really smoking and drinking at this time. At that point I was kind of tired of it, so my memory of that night is as vivid as if it were yesterday.

I remember this one dude in particular hanging around—someone I knew from back in the Joe's Garage days—and he's looking at me with these red, glassy eyes saying, "Yeah man, what's going awwwwwwwn ..." doing this fucking head-shuffle thing and I remember thinking, "Okay, let's see what this is all about." In my mind, I knew there was something amiss so I said, "Look, what the fuck are *you* on?" I asked him straight out.

"Oh, nothing, man," he said, but it turned out that he was the guy who brought it—heroin—in that night.

Now in those days I had a personal car and driver for me, my sister, and the rest of my family, and they would take anyone wherever they wanted to go. We were making the kind of money that we could afford to have limousines drive us wherever the fuck we wanted to.

So after the show, just as my sister is heading home, it suddenly hits the radio wire: "Philip Anselmo, singer with the rock band Pantera, has overdosed on heroin," and all I could think was, "Who the hell had *that* scoop?" It seemed that somebody knew quicker than they should have. Something about the whole night just didn't seem right to me.

When I went into the dressing room, it was a scene of total chaos: Phil was fucking blue because he had shot up after the show. Paramedics were called in and there was nothing I could do, although what I really wanted to do was beat the living shit out of Phil. As a compromise I took my rage out on the dressing room. I started throwing bowls of chips and chili around to release my anger. It was sickening and I was fucking furious. How the fuck could he have done this? How could he put all of our livelihoods at risk like this?

WALTER O'BRIEN

I knew that Phil was maybe taking a little too much pot and drinking too much, but not in a million years did I ever think he'd be on heroin. I actually quit that night in Dallas because I'd had firsthand experience—not of actually doing the drug, but of someone close to me dying as a result of it. So I had promised myself that I was never going to be an enabler for any band's drug problems or deal with any junkie. I had turned down some really great bands because I knew they were junkies, so I didn't want any part of it. We had a band meeting that night and they wanted me to go to the hospital and talk to him, and I said, "I'm not going *anywhere*. I'm not going to see him, I don't care and as far as I'm concerned, I'm here for you three guys for the next few days and then I quit." I did believe strongly that there was no Pantera without Phil, just like there was no Pantera without any one of Vinnie, Dime, or Rex, but I didn't want any part of this. Luckily they talked me out of it.

———————

The three of us met that night while Phil recovered in the hospital. Then the next morning, the boys picked me up in Dime's Cadillac, and we all went over to the hotel to confront the dude. He'd gotten out of the hospital already and had this girl with him who would die of an overdose shortly afterwards. It began to feel like there was some kind of dope plague going around.

We said to him, "What the fuck is this? What's going to happen? This could be the very fucking end of everything."

Walter was there with the other main management guy, Andy Gould, but neither of them did or said anything constructive. Because Walter had seen drug overdoses before, he'd just say, "Fuck you." That was his way of dealing. Management was no help at all. The best thing they could have done would have been to immediately put Phil in goddamn rehab, cancel the tour until he was clean, and then we could have all continued with what we were doing.

But that didn't happen.

Of course, when he was in front of us, Phil simply said, "I'm sorry, dudes. I really fucked up." What else could he say? But his response to the fact that the overdose was now public knowledge was more of a problem.

For some reason Phil wrote a confessional letter about his near-death experience, a public statement saying, "I saw no shining lights" or whatever the fuck he said—it's all well documented—and that was the dumbest thing he could have done, as far as I was concerned, because the moment he did that, he was labeled a junkie. Why would you do something like that? And why would management let him do it? They should have covered that shit up and that's all there is to it.

"Dude, why? We're *flying*," I said. "Money's through the fucking roof. What are you doing?"

Of course, Phil said it would never happen again, and we gave him the benefit of the doubt because when we examined the situation in the cold light of day, it wasn't like he was in a coma every fucking day. Even we would have noticed that. In fact I suspect he actually hadn't been using very long and had just been dabbling a little, but just happened to be unlucky and overdosed. Nobody's perfect, and there certainly aren't any saints in the business of rock 'n' roll, so of course people are occasionally going to have problems.

! # ⊕ *

DESPITE THE FACT that we were willing to move forward after the fiasco that night in Dallas, I'd be lying if I said that the thought of getting rid of Phil didn't cross our minds. But it only did so briefly and probably only as a knee-jerk response to what had happened, driven by our lack of understanding of and experience with what was actually going on.

Deep down, we knew that kicking out Phil would have been like ripping your heart out of your chest, or siphoning all the gas out of your car so that you can save the fucking car. There's no gasoline to make that car run, so you're keeping it for what? Totally pointless. We knew that to carry on without Phil would have been pointless, too. Even then and to this day he is one of the best front men in metal. Nobody commands an audience like he does, so we did carry on and after only one day off and our singer almost dead, Pantera was back and ready to hit Oklahoma.

! # ⊕ *

THE MAIN PART of the *Trendkill* tour featured three months on the road with White Zombie. While an element of trust had perhaps been lost after Phil's overdose, that feeling mellowed out over time, because when you're on tour you just have to get the job done no matter what. And in Phil's defense and to his great credit, he generally held it together thereafter. If he was still dabbling with heroin, it didn't affect the band.

! # ⊕ *

JEFF JUDD, one of my best friends since the early '90s when he worked as golf pro on a couple of courses in Ft. Worth, had always been a good guitar player. He was a fan of the band since the early days and he'd reached a time in his life where he wanted something different—he needed a career switch—so I offered him the chance to come out on the road with me as my bass tech.

JEFF JUDD (Rex's good friend and temporary bass tech)

Rex and I met through mutual friends and I'd played guitar since I was a kid. His bass tech had left after *Far Beyond Driven,* so he asked me to go out on the road. I didn't have any kids at the time, so it all worked out really well. Everything was pretty eye opening at the beginning, but the thing that I noticed most was that everyone seemed to actually *want* to work for Pantera. We did everything together just like a big family and they took the best care of everybody. We *stayed* at the same hotels as the band did, whereas all the other bands we went out with crews stayed at the Holiday Inn. Rex needed a friend out there, no doubt about that. There was definitely tension, mainly between the brothers and Phil, and it seemed to me that Rex was in the middle of it all. I'd met Dime and the rest of the band at the very end of the process of recording *Great Southern Trendkill* and when they heard I was going out on the road with Rex, they said, "Oh well, that'll be the end of your friendship." But if anything, it only made our friendship stronger.

————

Touring *Trendkill* also took us back down to South America during '97, this time touring with KISS, who were Dime and my heroes, and we were at the very top of our game. KISS were always a big-selling band down there and in that position where you want to make it count financially, they wanted the hottest opening band you can get and we just happened to be it at that time. We didn't see much of the KISS guys except a couple of nights when we all went to the Hard Rock Café in Buenos Aires.

This was a no-booze tour for them because Ace was back out with them for the first time, so they didn't go out much and neither did we, but while their reasons for not going out were driven by abstinence, ours were that we could cause utter chaos and carnage within the four walls of a hotel. So, we'd just go to the hotel bar or hang out in of one our rooms that had a bar.

I'll never forget my room in Santiago, Chile, The Intercontinental. When I opened the door for the first time, this dude dressed in a fucking tuxedo grabs my bag and starts putting all my clothes away in the closet while I'm thinking, "Who the fuck is this?"

Here I am in Santiago and I've got this killer room divided into all kinds of separate breakfast, living and sleeping areas, then another area that had a huge bouquet of fruit and a bunch of bottles of wine all set up for me by Warner Brothers, Chile *and* I've got this guy. What a fucking trip! After he'd put all my shit away, the guy's still standing there.

So I called Jeff and said, "Dude, come down to my room. There's this guy just standing there." He goes, "What do you mean?"

"I don't know; he's just standing like he wants a tip or something," I told him. So Jeff comes down and we both look at this guy and say, "So dude, what do you actually *do*?"

"Oh, I'm your personal butler," the guy says, so I go, "Fuck! Well go get us a bottle of Jack Daniels and start pouring them. Pour them up, baby!" And that's what he did. In fact he did anything we wanted. If we wanted to get something to eat, he'd just go and get it. He'd do laundry and the whole bit. It was fucking wild. We had a good time with this guy in the end and it turned out that all the other guys each had a butler, too.

JEFF JUDD

Rex's room had a huge fruit platter that was three feet wide and piled up two feet tall with papayas, all kinds of stuff. Next thing Dime shows up with a rain stick, a three-foot long hollowed-out piece of wood with beads inside that makes a sound like rain falling. He sees the fruit platter and says, "Pitch one of those over!" and he swings at it and smashes it across the room. Then the baseball game was *on*. The room looked like a fruit salad. The walls, the ceiling, everything was covered, and this butler dude had gone by then, but we had his number, which we used when we needed the room cleaned up. All the picture frame glass was broken so we ended up taking all the glass out so they looked like pictures again. He washed all the walls down, took all the broken stuff away, and we gave him a hundred bucks and headed off down the road. We never even got a call on it.

We were getting a lot of attention on that KISS tour, so much so that during the KISS sets fans started chanting our name between their songs—"Pan-te-ra, Pan-te-ra!" that kind of thing. That really pissed them off. We'd climb up on the scaffolding so we could watch them play from the side of the show and the second time this chanting deal happened, I looked at the guys and said, "We're down, we gotta go." And then we left the gig.

! # ⊕ *

IT'S NO SURPRISE that the South American fans dug us. We were on it as far as our live performance went. *Really* on it. Ferocious at times. I like to pride myself in the fact that I missed very few notes. And when I say "'missed," I mean *misplayed,* not hitting wrong ones; it'd be something about how my fingers attack a note, really miniscule details that nobody else could possibly notice. But *I* noticed.

There's nights where I might over-slide a note or two, too, but that's no big deal, that's just rock 'n' roll. Then there's nights when I might want to play kind of punk rock—not be as tight as usual—and there's certain songs where you can get away with it and others where you can't. I didn't always want to be Mr. Tight Man and have everything sound the same night after night. Maybe that's my lab band, freestyle mentality coming through.

Every night I was looking for a different challenge, too. Vinnie Paul was like a metronome, almost to the point where there was no variation, so I had to make up my own parts to make it entertaining, because if you play the same thing two hundred and something nights a year, it gets real fucking boring.

The actual sets we played on any given night mostly depended on Phil's voice—where he wanted to go and what he thought he could do with it—and that was something we had to take one day at a time. So three hours before the show, we'd know more or less what the set list was going to be. I'd get in there in the late afternoon and work through the list with Phil to see how he was feeling, and then I'd bring in the boys and say, "How's this going to work?"

Or on other days Vinnie and I would put something together ourselves based on where we thought Phil's voice was, but usually everything hinged on him. Understandably, Phil had nights where he had problems with his voice, but any singer is going to have that, no matter who you are, and it especially happens to the great ones. But because he was so great, he had his own subtle ways of getting around any voice issues he might have had. Maybe he wouldn't sing the top notes or not sing a particular note at all but either way, when you consider how many fucking nights we'd play, in the scheme of things he didn't have many problems.

The Pantera set list also depended on which songs we'd rehearsed. At the beginning of pre-production we'd have a list of probably twenty-five songs that would form the bulk of our general rotation, but occasionally someone would say, "Tomorrow let's do *this* song. Everybody think about it tonight, listen to it and then come in tomorrow and make it work."

If we were playing a place two nights in a row, which we occasionally did, we'd have to change the set because we didn't want to do the same thing twice for the kids who came to see both shows. That would have been cheating them. Depending on how things were going with a particular crowd sometimes we'd go off on different tangents, do little ditties so that we didn't get stale.

WE ALL IMPROVISED individually where we could and on the occasions when Dime decided to go off on one, it was always fucking awesome to behold from the other side of the stage. Me? I just laid down the low end and he could play anything he wanted to over the top, no matter what I had going on. Sometimes I'd get goose bumps from some of the stuff he did. Dime's playing never ceased to blow me away, so much so that I'd occasionally go over and give him a kiss!

We'd usually critique right after the show. Ask questions like "What could have been better?," "Was the tempo of this or that song right?," or "Does this song fit in?" By that time we had so much adrenaline going that we could sit in the dressing room for hours afterwards, drinking and getting loaded. In later years when we had more space, Phil was usually in another dressing room, but the three of us would analyze every fucking thing over and over and that's why we were always such a tight live band.

We refined our pre-show routine over the years, too. We'd have hospitality rooms, game rooms, all kinds of shit laid on for us, but apart from playing video games, reading a magazine, or watching football on TV, there isn't a whole lot to do on show days once you're at the venue. It would have been easy to get loaded, but for the most part, we started drinking usually an hour before the show. We'd have a few shots and the whole bit.

Then that hour turned into an hour and a half before the show, which eventually turned into two hours, and so on.

Then sometimes me and Dime would just get up in the morning, say "fuck it," and just start drinking. And then when it came to getting up on stage *those* nights we'd somehow fly by the seat of our asses. How we did it I have no idea, but we played some of the best shows of our career in that state. I was never so fucked up that I didn't know where I was or anything or was staggering around on stage, stumblin' and grumblin' as I like to call it, but there were a few nights where definitely I came off afterwards and thought, "How the fuck did I do that?" But there weren't that many nights like that and I never ever missed a show. Amazing statistics when you consider how many fucking dates we played. I'm not saying every night was the best night we ever played, that's not realistic, but Pantera at 80 percent was like another band's hundred and fifty percent.

! # ⊕ *

I REMEMBER MANY OCCASIONS when Dime and I used to get off the bus in the morning when we pulled into a new town. He and I would be fucking *green* from drinking all night but it never even entered our minds not to play that night. On those days, "Here we go again, buddy," was all I would say to him as we walked across the parking lot to the venue, arm in arm. We knew what had to be done.

WALTER O'BRIEN

When Rex had too much to drink he'd maybe get a little ornery but he'd also get really talkative. In fact he always wanted to talk to me at four in the morning, when I was exhausted and dead asleep. He'd want to spend three hours talking business and I would be feeling like saying, "Oh, my God, please leave me alone!" But at least he cared about his own career. Nobody else ever wanted to talk.

———

I got really fucking sick one night in Atlanta touring *Far Beyond Driven,* but it had nothing to do with alcohol. I had strep throat with a hundred and four degree fever and we were playing a place that must have been a hundred and twenty degrees. It was all I could do to just stand up. I was in the hospital before the show, got up, played the show, and went straight into an ambulance back to the hospital; that's how sick I was and still we only cut the show short by fifteen minutes. That was the only stage time I ever missed.

MY DRINKS OF CHOICE were beer and whiskey—although in later years I took a liking to red wine—and there would be nights where my bass tech would have a trash can at my side of the stage, just in case. Sometimes, I'd think, "Fuck it, Goddamn, I've got to catch up," so I'd drink another beer real fast just before we went on and so the trash can was there so I could fucking chunk if I had to. And then I'd have another shot and be fine.

This was all Jeff's job, as well as changing all the strings on the basses, making sure that all my amps are powered, all the hook-ups set up and the whole bit. And of course he kept my mini-bar stocked. I usually took about six basses on stage at a time and all I had to do

was take the guitar I was playing off my shoulder, he'd hand me another, switch the wireless packs over, and I was good to go. Depending on where you're playing, guitars and basses go out of tune a lot.
If you're playing in a fucking hockey rink—and we played in a lot of
them—where they just board up the ice, it could be really cold and
Jeff would be tuning my basses all night long. And if the venue's really humid the bass necks would seem to bend.

WE WENT TO AUSTRALIA in late '96 and the process of getting there
was a complete nightmare. Vinnie, Dime, and the rest had already
gone on before us, so I was scheduled to fly out with Phil, his assistant, and Big Val. So I get to LAX and in those days we had fans everywhere, so someone at the airport would always recognize me, shoot
me into a little buggy, and say, "So, Mr. Brown, where would you like
to go?"

On this occasion they put me and Big Val in a buggy and took us
to one of these waiting lounges called something like the Admiral's
Club. We walk in there and I see Phil sitting with the comedian Don
Rickles. So for the next couple of hours before we fly, he sits and gets
scotch drunk with Don as our pre-flight entertainment. You can't
even imagine the crazy shit that was coming out of his mouth. I
wasn't drinking at the time, but Big Val had a shitload of Valium on
him.

Predictably, by the time we got to our first class seats on Qantas
Airlines, Phil was completely wasted. It was very high-end—champagne and caviar for the whole trip—and Phil's looking around, pan-
icking that we're not sitting together and the whole bit. I asked some
guy if he would move, but he just had to have his fucking window
seat or something, so I just said, "'No big deal, I'll just sit wherever
I've been assigned." I was just trying to be nice, but this guy was being a real fucking asshole about it for whatever reason.

Then Phil says to him, "You know what, you're a fucking dick" and that just escalated things, and Phil started to become all paranoid thinking everyone was looking at him. "Fuck you, don't look at me, fuck *you*, don't look at me!" he'd say to everyone. Then he wanted to get his Walkman or something to use during the flight and they wouldn't let him get into his luggage. "Settle down, dude," I told him, "It's really not that big of a deal."

Phil had a history of being a handful on flights. We'd fly places and he'd kind of nod out, face down in his food. That happened all the time. So, I'd grab his head. "What the fuck are you doing?" he'd say. "Dude, I'm tired of looking at you with your face in a plate," I'd tell him.

Meanwhile, downstairs in coach class, Big Val was throwing a fucking commotion about something—he couldn't find his head-phones or his seat wasn't big enough, some stupid shit like that—so they ended up throwing us all off the plane. They got the cops in LAX to come and get us and the whole bit.

Back in the terminal we had to go all the way back through security. I had to put a call in to someone who could think of something fast that would get us out of this mess, but Sykes and them were already Down Under. I didn't know who I could call. So as we're going back through the security line, they find all this Valium on Big Val; they detained him and escorted us out of there. But Phil and I still had to find a way to get on another flight.

We had to get all the way across LAX—and it's a huge fucking airport. We could see the United Airlines terminal straight across from where we were dumped off, but it was going to take forever to get all the way over there in a cab.

So we just started hauling ass across this field in the middle of LAX—it was probably part of the goddamn runway, who knows, and Phil didn't have a suitcase either. He had everything in fucking *boxes*. For some reason that's how he liked to do it, and it should be said that Phil is pretty eccentric in that respect. And he always had prob-lems with luggage. On what seemed like every trip, everybody else's bag would get through, but Phil's wouldn't show up. So he would just throw a fucking fit. I'm philosophical about that kind of thing, so I used to say to him, "Come on man, you're still breathing. It's not the end of the world." So from then on he started taking boxes and carry-on shit.

I didn't question it at this point either, I just thought, "You want to do your shit in boxes, do it in boxes. Fuck it."

So I'm trying to carry his shit as well as my bags, and by the time we get to the United desk we're both just covered with sweat. Not just that, I'd snapped a fingernail in half carrying Phil's stuff, but because it was my right hand, I could tape it up and it wouldn't be a problem for when I had to play a bass.

So we finally get booked on this plane in roach class but the problem was that it was going to fucking New Zealand and not Australia. When we get there, after too many hours of traveling, we find out that U.S. Customs had called New Zealand Customs, presumably to have us checked out for carrying drugs.

Now by this point I'm fucking *pissed*. I'd flown double-digit hours to the wrong country in coach class, when I *could* have been living in seventeen hours of luxury in a full-blown champagne and caviar wet dream that was pure intoxication.

That was a fantasy.

The reality was different. They took us into a room at the airport in New Zealand and stripped us fucking nude.

And it was a full strip search, rubber gloves up the ass and the whole bit. Phil and I weren't carrying, so there wasn't a problem for us. Big Val had all the Valium on him, and he was probably still detained at LAX!

After another short flight from New Zealand, we finally got to our hotel in Australia. I called Vince and said, "Fuck Val, he's fired, man."

I thought he should have handled the situation better—that's what we pay him to do—but Vinnie wanted him (a) because he hated confrontation of any kind and (b) because he needed a security guard. He was right about the second part, probably. We *all* needed a security guard when it came to controlling the crowd at shows, and Val was admittedly really good at that. Although he flew out a couple of days later, nobody really spoke to him and this was the beginning of the end for Big Val. He was starting to think he was a bigger rock star than us.

! # ⊕ *

DESPITE THESE PROBLEMS, I liked Australia as a place to visit, but it seemed like their economy was always in the shitter, almost to the extent that it cost us money to go and play there, even though we knew we'd most likely get it all back in future record sales. But we just felt that if we were going to be over on that side of the world, we might as well hit everywhere we could, so that included New Zealand, Australia, Japan, and also wilder places like Seoul, Korea.

! # ⊕ *

THERE WAS A NEAR-RIOT at one of the gigs we played in Australia. We came out after a show in Sydney and the fans were all over this parking garage outside. There were thousands of people. It was fucking insane. Should have made a video out of it, that's how killer it was. Apparently they'd charged at a barricade fence, knocked it over, and spilled into this parking lot, just to get closer to us.

JEFF JUDD

We were in Japan on the *Trendkill* tour and we found this toy store that was six stories tall. Bobby, a band assistant, and I go in there and we buy these battery BB guns that shoot plastic pellets. We go back to Rex and the guys and

they said, "We gotta have us a war here with these guns."
We had an entire floor of the Hilton, so we get these
things charging and go to dinner. After we got back after
a few drinks, we pick these guns up and Rex fires the first
shot at a beer can that was sitting on the counter and this
thing splits the can in half. We were like, "All right, this is
not a game anymore." Then Dime starts shooting out all
the wine glasses in the wine bar that served the floor of
our hotel, then the pictures get riddled up, then all the light
bulbs got shot out. There was glass everywhere. By the
morning, all our bedrooms are shot up. I'll never forget
Dime calling down to the front desk, putting on a Japanese
accent asking for light bulbs. The guy at the desk asked
him what kind he meant, and at that point Dime said in his
Texas accent, "Goddamn hundred-watters son, they look
better when they blow!" So, they sent someone up and
Dime wouldn't let them in the room because of all the
damage. The final total on all of it ended up being about
seventeen thousand dollars, and it ended up being a big
deal as well as a big disrespectful thing there. The
promoter—the same guy who first brought the Beatles to
Japan—ended up having to write a letter to the consulate
and we were banned from every Hilton in Japan.

———————

! # ⊕ *

TOURING *TRENDKILL* was a fucking blur, man, a *total* blur. On the
way back from wherever we were last—maybe Japan—we stopped
off for a break in Maui. We often did this kind of thing on the way
back from overseas trips, and Hawaii was a favorite of mine because
I'd proposed to Belinda there back in '94 and I loved surfing.

We were meant to stay there for seven days and the wives were going to come out and join us for some of that time, but me and Dime ended up staying there for two and a half weeks. We had rented cars but never used them; we just stayed at the hotel. They had shuttles to little islands, and Dime and I made our own little spot on the beach and sat there chilling. We'd get up at about one and have a drink and a sandwich or whatever. It was a perfect escape.

! # ⊕ *

SOMETIME DURING ALL THIS, Jerry Cantrell had sent me a tape of about eleven songs that he wanted me to play on. Me, him, and Sean Kinney, and my first thought was, "Yeah, this is exactly what I need."

Here was a chance to broaden my horizons a little bit while also getting away from all the Pantera band issues. Of course I'd known Jerry since '87 and was a huge Alice in Chains fan, so I went up to Sausalito, California, for about a month, rehearsed, came home, and then went *back* there to record a bunch of tracks which were going to be produced by Toby Wright, who'd worked on a couple of Alice in Chains records.

Well, it wasn't long before I got into a fight with Toby.

He'd keep saying shit like, "Oh, you can't play it like that," to which I replied "Dude, Jerry invited me down to play so I'm going to play whatever the fuck I want to, understand?"

Scotty Olson was Toby's engineer on the project, and he's just a sweetheart of a guy—he played guitar in Heart for years—and he made me feel comfortable because he'd worked with our producer Terry Date in the past. So because I felt like he was an ally, my attitude to Toby was very much like, "If you don't like it, get the fuck out of the room. I'm going to lay my shit down and that's the way it's going to go."

Amazingly, Toby Wright *still* calls me from time to time saying stuff like, "Hey man, I'm looking for a gig."

"You're a piece of shit," is about all I'll offer in reply.

Jerry was in no position at that point either due to his excessive drug use. Without going into too much detail, let's just say I would go past his place from time to time and see his dog chained up with no food in the bowl for three fucking days, and that indicated to me that maybe something was seriously wrong. It felt like I was leaving one for another. Crazy shit.

CHAPTER 14
THE 'TUDE

The Toby Wright fiasco was an example of the scrappy character I'd been since I was a kid. Yes, I could handle myself if I had to, but I'd also developed a really strong bark and that was almost always enough to get people to back down. I nurtured that as I got older to the point that whenever I walked into a room, I did so as if to say, "This is my room," no questions asked. Dime, Phil, and I were all like that in our different ways. Whenever we walked into a room our presence was noted. *Duly* noted. We were united and you did not fuck with us.

As a general principle, I guarantee that when I first walk into a room I can set the tone for whatever the outcome's going to be, just by changing the expression on my face. When I walk in I make sure that everybody knows it's my room and you don't fuck with me, and then after that we start talking like any normal people. Of course I'll always show manners and respect, but at that initial point of entry, it's as if I'm walking in there as part of a street gang. We wanted people to think, "Here's these crazy fuckers from Texas. They drink a shitload of booze and they'll kick your fucking ass." Even though me and Dime were tiny in physical stature, we more than made up for it in attitude.

It might surprise you to know that this attitude is more important to me than going up onstage and hitting a lick. I'm serious. It shows who you are more than *anything*. If you walk in there all smiley or all scared, people just will not take you seriously and you will lose any argument or negotiation before it even starts. Consequently, I've never been starstruck in my entire life. I can't afford to do that. It would put me in a position of weakness, and since childhood I haven't liked that place.

At times it has not been easy to not be fazed by certain scenarios, because throughout my career I've been in situations that even I think are pretty fucking cool, like hanging out with Ozzy, smoking a joint and the whole bit. Had people calling me on the phone that you just wouldn't expect, and these are guys that I've idolized, worshipped even, since I was a kid. I got the chance to meet Jimmy Page in London once, and beforehand I didn't even *want* to meet him— what if he turned out to be a total tool? I just didn't want to know that. But it did make me think about how *I* am when people come up to *me*. Let's say I'm in a bad mood—a little irritated maybe—and then when people come up to me, maybe they want to know if *I'm* a total tool. That really made me think about other people's perception of me because I realized that strangers probably have a certain level of expectation about how I am. Unfortunately a lot of people in the public eye get reputations for being assholes, so my thinking was always to surprise them by showing that I'm not, rather than confirming their preconceived suspicion that I am.

That's not always easy though because I come from the old school of rock 'n' roll, which involves trying to live just like Keith Richards. Lots of guys in this business try to do that. Slash, Nikki Sixx, they all fought hard to emulate Keith, but by their own admission they never got there. I still have that vision in my brain, but I've got to get rid of it because, as you'll find out later, I can't drink anymore, which kind of defeats the point. In any case, if you read Keith's book you'll see that it's not like he went out and partied every night for his entire career either. He didn't do that. He knew how to balance his life and that's probably why he's still playing at sixty-something years old.

THE PRESS WANTED to give Dime this whole certain aura after his death, but really that was an old wive's tale. He was a charismatic guy, no doubt about it, but one who could make you feel like you're the most amazing person on the planet, just by being in his company. He entertained himself by doing crazy shit and by getting you to do crazy shit, too, but you couldn't help but just love the cat, even though he pissed me off so many times that I can't even count.

Darrell was always the culprit of practical jokes, and with him the camera was always on while they played out, so it's no wonder we made three home videos of crazy shit and the fans bought it. In fact a lot of times the fans were in them.

To relieve tedium while we were on the road, Darrell would always come up with something: cards, dice, or shooting fireworks under somebody in a moving vehicle, so there was never a dull moment.

We even drove the bus a few times to relieve the boredom, and I wasn't always in great shape behind the wheel when I did it. The bus driver would sit and get smashed with Dime in the back regularly, so somebody had to steer the ship, and I often drove the bus from one town to the next.

WALTER O'BRIEN

When it came to making the home videos, Dime thought he could direct. I knew he couldn't. Also, some of the stuff he had in there was outrageous—material he had because he kept the camera rolling backstage. There were acts involving Heineken bottles that you just wouldn't believe. It was basically pornography. I used to say to him, "Look, I know that you think this is funny and these incidents really do happen but Warner Brothers are not in the business of selling hardcore pornography." Did he get it? Of course not.

————————

Our profile was boosted further—if that's possible—in '97 when we were invited on the Ozzfest tour—its first proper year—and that was the beginning of a great relationship with Sharon and Ozzy Osbourne. We were the biggest metal band out there at the time, so what were they going to do? It was obvious what they had to do: Get Pantera on the bill.

Ozzfest *had* to pay. If they were going to do this thing, it *had* to be successful.

WALTER O'BRIEN

Ozzy was always out there touring and he always had a tradition of putting out younger bands to open for him, incredibly sensible marketing on his part. We kept trying to hound them and hound them to take us out, as did every manager of every other heavy metal band in the world. We tried and tried, and then finally Sharon said, "Because so many bands are always trying to tour with us, we're going to do Ozzfest, then that way we can take a bunch of them out and call it a festival." So they took us out and afterwards I made a point of sending her a thank you letter. One day when I was on the phone with her a few weeks later she said, "I have to tell you something. Your letter is on the wall above my computer in my office." I said, "That's tremendous; I'm really honored, but why?"

And she said, "Ozzy saw it and he said 'In all my years
of bringing out young groups, this is the first time any
manager thought to send us a letter of thanks.'" I'm not
going to say that they got the Ozzfest slots because of that
letter, but it certainly didn't hurt, let's put it that way. I
don't think Ozzy could have gotten away with touring
every year for seven straight years without something like
Ozzfest to carry it.

———

Although he had sold millions of records during the '90s, nobody
in the industry really gave a shit about Ozzy at this particular point,
so he badly needed a reinvention of some kind. Sharon had tried to
get him on Lollapalooza and they just wouldn't have him.

I would imagine they said something like, "Go fuck yourself. We
don't want Ozzy Osbourne, the washed-up old Black Sabbath turd"
type of thing.

But Pantera always had a good relationship with him—management, crew, and everyone else—and that sense of harmony just escalated, as did the money we got paid to show up. We'd get up there,
play forty-five minutes to an hour, and get paid *beaucoup* for doing
so. It was so easy to get up and do because it was day on, day off, and
during the off days the promoters set us up with free golf at the most
killer courses in the whole of America. I was living in a house right
on Rolling Hills Country Club in Arlington by this time, so my golf
game wasn't at all shit. In fact I was taking the piss out of Sykes and
all these guys in those days.

Guy Sykes was one of my best friends, sure, but he was also our
tour manager, in charge of four individual fucking psychopaths, and
we certainly made his life difficult at times. His responsibility was to
make everything as comfortable as possible for us on the road, and
in all honesty he was good-spirited, given some of the shit we put
him through. He really was a trooper. He had to be because Dime
would come up with something fucking crazy every night: grass

skirts, top hats, and the whole fucking thing, and Sykes would have no choice but to go sort it out. Then I said to him, "I'm not going on stage unless I've got one of those cocktail umbrellas in my drink every night." So they went to a Party Hut and bought a whole case so I could never bitch about it again. I used to fuck with Sykes all the time about that kind of shit.

On the on days during Ozzfest, Sharon showed she could drink like any of us. She'd come into our dressing room just to get fucked up, probably because Ozzy was out of his fucking mind most of the time. This was during the time he was in and out of rehab. But when he was sober, he was one of the sharpest dudes I've ever met in my whole life, and nothing like you've seen on TV. In front of the cameras he puts on this confused persona, but he definitely has it all together.

At one show he had this trailer sitting out backstage somewhere, and he says to someone, "Send the Pantera boys over."

So me and Dime jumped in a golf cart and went over, and he's sitting there with his robe on and his fucking balls are hanging out.

First thing he says is, "You buoooys want to smoke a joint?" in that thick Birmingham accent of his. We're thinking, "What did you say?" You just don't say no to Ozzy.

"You guys want a drink?" is his next offer.

"No thanks Ozzy, wait … of *course* we're going to have a drink with you." Remember, we were as notorious as fucking Mötley Crüe back then even though we weren't using a whole bunch of coke and all that shit. But we *could* drink some liquor.

Yeah, well as much as I admired him and as happy I was to have a drink with him, I draw the line at staring at his or anyone else's balls, so eventually I said to him, "Dude, can you please put your fuckin' balls away. I don't want to stare at your gum all night." He ignored me.

"Godfather of Metal would you mind covering up the huevos?" I asked again.

"Aww fuck you mate." Ozzy didn't give a shit.

! # ⊕ *

THIS WAS THE BEGINNING of some really good years with the Ozzy guys, and one of the reasons it worked out so well is because we were always very respectful of bands that we admired. We were always very cordial and *never* stepped on anyone's toes. At least I hope we didn't. They definitely helped our careers to a certain point, but it also got to the level where it was detrimental because of Sharon's drinking while her man was trying to get sober. It just became expected that we were going to do this thing every year and we just got a little bored of the same routine.

We got asked out on three more cycles of the Ozzfest Tour, the last of them in 2003 when I was with Down, and by that time I had a pretty close friendship with Ozzy. Sharon had just been diagnosed with cancer, and you could just tell that he wasn't taking it all very well. He took me in at one point and said, "I'm fuckin' lost, man. I don't know what the fuck I'm going to do."

Because it felt like I'd gained a certain amount of his respect as a result of doing all those tours with him, I felt comfortable offering my support on a human level, so I simply said, "If there's anything I can say or do to help, just let me know. My thoughts and prayers are with you."

CHAPTER 15

SABBATH AND DOWN WITH THE GAMBLER

*O*fficial Live was also released in '97 and was composed of a bunch of live recordings from previous tours, recorded from the soundboard on DAT machines that we took on the road. We were known as a live band, so it was time that we made a live record. We played so many shows and the whole bit so we had all this material already on tape; it was just a case of someone going through it all, going through the process of finding the best versions of the songs we wanted on there. We also added a couple of new studio tracks that we recorded on our own, without the help of a producer, back at Dime's house.

I was working on Cantrell's stuff most of the time anyway and only flew back to Dallas once to do the bass tracks for the new songs. I don't remember overdubbing anything else on the live album; it was just a case of getting the mix right. Maybe we upped the crowd noise a little bit or fixed a couple of Phil's vocals here and there, but everybody does that. There's no true live record that I know of out there.

WALTER O'BRIEN

We were getting so many problems of "Phil said this onstage, Phil said that," that I said, "Listen, I want every show recorded on tape" because I was sick of people saying anything they want, like, "Well, Phil said 'come onstage and beat up a security guard,' etc." The problem was that Phil often did say these kinds of things. Anyway I had given the sound guy instructions, saying, "Record the show and anytime he says something like that, burn the tape immediately." So that way we'd have a bunch of live shows with nothing incriminating on them. We also kept getting offered to do live shows on the radio, live broadcasts, and these guys just would not agree to anything. I kept saying, "You're the best live act I have ever seen. We have to take advantage of that." The networks were begging us to do live shows nationally but the guys said, "No, we want to mix it, we want to record it," and I said, "You can't, it's live, that's the whole point." But they wouldn't do it. Finally we convinced them to use DAT to make high-quality, multi-track recordings for the cost of a couple of tapes and so we recorded the shows. Also, everyone was starting to run out of money anyway so we said, "Time for the live record!" Just like everyone else in the world.

At some point in '98 I went down to New Orleans, just to get out of Dallas for a while. I needed a boy's weekend out but it turned into something completely different. Phil said, "Hey man, do you want to come and write some songs?" and of course I was like "Sure, cool." So I got to Phil's old house that's in the middle of New Orleans proper—Colbert Street in fact—and it was just this little-bitty small place that was the first place he ever bought when Pantera first started making money.

So when I walk in there, here's Kirk Windstein, here's Jimmy Bower, and here's Pepper Keenan, so I just thought, "Cool man! This is happening!" And they said, "Do you wanna come and jam downstairs?" I was still unaware I was being auditioned to be the Down bass player. Phil had a jam room in the downstairs garage area and he also had himself a real haunted house. There was foam, skeletons, cobwebs, and all kinds of crazy shit that you walked through. The house was built on stilts, so the garage was underneath and he had a fucking pentagram painted red on the bottom of his swimming pool.

I said, "I don't have a fucking bass with me," because I hadn't planned on playing when I was in town. Anyway, Phil had this bass for me to use and an old, fried amp, and we started jamming and all this stuff just started coming out of us in the most organic way. There were so many memorable moments during those sessions, but the one that sticks out most is the song "Lies."

Pepper came in with this jazz thing and I pitched in instinctively with a killer jazz bass line, something totally different from all the heavy metal stuff we were used to. I felt we'd touched on not only new territory for the band, but also a style of music that resonated with me from my childhood days playing in jazz bands. It really was inspiring.

Down was rooted in New Orleans, which is a hugely diverse cultural melting pot. You therefore have jazz, rhythm and blues, rock, metal, and sludge all merged together in one big gumbo. I'm from

Texas and I've known those other New Orleans guys for as long as I've known Philip, and when we get in the same room together, we just sit there and put all of our individual influences and all our tastes together and see what comes out at the end.

As it happens, we wrote a lot of that second Down record there and then—at least six or seven tracks—and for me the diversification into new territory was (a) what I needed and (b) something I wanted to see through to the point of making a record, but only when a suitable gap in the Pantera schedule opened up.

In '98 or '99, after a short tour to promote *Official Live*, we also went out on the Black Sabbath reunion tour for nine months. It was great and they paid us a fucking lot of money to do it, and when cash like that comes, you do not turn it down. It also felt like we were taking part in a significant event, too, because it was the first time they'd played together since Ozzy had left the band in 1979. It was primarily in large arenas—a domain that we knew we ruled—and we tore it up every fucking night.

Even if you're Black Sabbath, you don't go *after* Pantera. You'd be stupid to even try. Even with Phil in a drunken state—and that was hit or miss in those days—you still don't do it because the three of us were so fucking tight. That Sabbath tour was probably the best we ever were live. It was really game on. We had toned our stage stuff down a lot—just put up some barbed wire to try to get away from that whole big Marshall stack look—so we really didn't use a bunch of cabinets on that tour, we just got up there and played the music instead of relying on special effects.

WALTER O'BRIEN

The band was really back in the game on the Sabbath reunion tour. As good as they always played in the small clubs, they were one of those bands that really kicked butt when they got in front of that many people.

Then when we were done I'd sit there and watch Sabbath every single night, and it was fucking unbelievable. Of course I met Geezer and got to know him pretty well, and near the end of the tour he invited me over to his dressing room, where we just sat and went through about three bottles of red wine, almost like a wine tasting, while we sat and just talked shit together. Geezer has a very dry sense of humor, too, and now that we're more familiar, he likes to call me "Rox." Funny.

We've done tons of promotional stuff together since then. I've interviewed him for bass magazines and it's just great to even be in the same room with him and for him to even recognize who I am. As well as being what I'd now call a friend, he's also an extremely influential bass player. It's all in the way he attacks the string with his fingers that makes him so great, I reckon. He kind of slaps the string with his right hand and instead of picking down and keeping his hand straight; he kind of moves his hand around and does all this crazy shit … while hitting every single note with his left hand. There's just nobody like him.

WHILE THERE WERE good aspects to that Sabbath trip—lots of them, even—there was also some bad personal shit going down among us. The tension among the band members was as high as it's ever been, and I was getting to the point of not wanting to deal with any of it.

Vinnie was the biggest problem.

On countless nights, Dime and I would be sitting on the bus trying to have a hot meal when Vinnie would invite all these young-looking chicks back to the bus hoping he could get a piece of ass. The crew had already had their pick of these girls anyway, and it was just so awkward sitting there watching Vinnie's pathetic attempts to get laid. Half the time he'd pass out drunk, and that just left Dime and I to deal with all his bullshit and pick up all the pieces.

You need to understand that Vinnie is just a strange person—that's all there is to it—and it's either his way or the highway. I think he got most of that asshole-ishness from his old man, because in many ways they are very much alike. Vinnie's was always all about the "party, party, party!" and "eat that pussy!" type of shit—to the extent that he thought he was fucking David Lee Roth. And him a *drummer,* can you imagine? But the truth is that he only got laid maybe one out of ten times and that's if he was lucky. Being in a platinum-selling band is meant to be a head start when you're trying to score with chicks, but he negated that by having no idea whatsoever how to treat or approach a woman. He'd just walk up and immediately start *groping* them, so it was no surprise that his strike rate was so pitiful. He acted like meeting him was a sexual audition and that just turned them off straightaway.

And as if that wasn't bad enough, when he didn't get laid (ninety percent of the time, I'd estimate) he was the most miserable fucking guy on the planet. I just couldn't live with him. He'd walk in the room in the morning and I'd just *know.* He'd be all snappy and pissed off with everyone and there was nothing anyone could do to change his mood. That became really boring.

PHIL HAD MOVED off the main bus back in '95 and travelled with his assistant, trainer, and the whole bit, so I eventually confided in him.

"I've got to get off their bus, man, all Vinnie's shit is driving me fucking crazy."

He said, "Dude, you can have the front lounge of my bus, I never use it."

Thank fuck he agreed to that. So I made the decision to move off Vinnie and Darrell's bus to Phil's place, and that apparently seemed to cause a whole load of bitching and resentment. Dime particularly took it really personally, which at that time did not even register with me. I was too concerned with extracting myself. I didn't give a fuck either, and if anything was ever said about it, it wasn't said to me. I was so worn down anyway that all I cared about was that I got some peace and because the atmosphere on Phil's bus was a bit more serene and adult, it was a world away from Vinnie's immature bullshit. Dime was probably just jealous because he knew he now had to fend for himself.

RITA HANEY

Darrell felt really unhappy about Rex riding on the bus with Phil. He also thought it was really out of character because Phil and Rex never really used to hang out. They just didn't have things in common. When Phil came to town, he would stay with us because he and Darrell had a relationship that had been formed since day one. So it all seemed bizarre that Phil and Rex were buddies all of a sudden.

———

! # ⊕ *

I ALWAYS LIKED TO GAMBLE. Gambled all the time when we were on the road and casinos were a big part of Pantera's deal. Me, Vinnie, Dime, and some of the crew would hit them. But never Phil. He never gambled and hated those places. But if there was a casino within two miles of where we were, the tour buses often got diverted to wherever that was. I was really into playing craps for a while and I won around twenty-two thousand in one night, just sitting there playing. But like most gamblers, I didn't always win. And unlike most gamblers, I'll tell you about the times when I lost.

I knew the Maloof brothers, who owned casinos in Vegas, basketball teams, and the whole bit, because they went to school with a guy who I knew from a bar down the street from me called Hetfield's. I got to know them pretty well, to the point that anytime I went to Vegas they would lay on a room for me somewhere. And by a room, I mean a real nice, huge suite. So my assistant and I took a trip to Vegas sometime during the Sabbath tour in '99; we checked in at the Aladdin where they had a VIP kind of setting, planning to play on the marker I had there.

We went down to the tables at about seven in the evening and started playing on the five thousand dollar marker I had. At this point I'd probably had a couple of drinks but you could still just about read my signature. I immediately lose the five grand and think, "Okay, I've *got* to get back up again," so what else can I do but take another marker out for the same amount.

Well this dollar-chasing went on until four or five in the morning, and when I woke up the next day, I got a bill under the door for twenty thousand dollars, and when I looked it over I could see that by the last of the five thousand dollar markers, you could barely decipher my signature at all. The reason for that was that we had taken breaks during the evening, had bottles of Crown Royal, champagne sent up to the room, so that had added to the markers and pumped up the overall bill. What now? I was in the hole for twenty grand after one bad night. Of course I didn't have that kind of cash on me, but I also knew that casinos will normally allow debtors thirty days before they start getting stressed about getting their money back. I needed a plan and pretty soon I came up with one. It was risky, sure, and reliant on my luck turning from pure shit into solid gold, but it seemed to be worth a try.

Thankfully the bus driver on our bus also liked to gamble. Phil didn't care because he was always wasted in the back, so me, the bus driver, and Phil's assistant decided to go into all the Native American casinos along our route to try and win the twenty grand back. The tour was due to end up in Seattle, so I figured we had almost the entire West Coast from San Diego northwards to get lucky.

So the bus driver mapped everything out, got all the places located and in conference with everyone who was going to play, I said,

"Look, here's the plan. Everybody walks in with three hundred bucks. If you want me to bankroll you, I'll bankroll you, but you have to pay me back the three hundred when we're done." Then I added, "We have *one hour* to play with three hundred bucks. If you lose it, you're out."

So after every show for a week and a half, we'd mosey out of whatever town we happened to be in, and go to one of these pre-identified casinos to put the plan into action. We were playing straight blackjack, strictly by the rules. We'd gotten ourselves a book that told you what to hit on, depending on what the banker is showing and what to do about it. It was basically a cheat-sheet of how to play the game strategically.

I set up the table like something out of *Ocean's Eleven*. Every person had a specific job to do. I had a guy on first base, another guy on fourth, and I played the two middle slots. That way I figured we had all the options covered. To be as sharp as possible I eased back on the drinking too—only one drink an hour—so that way I was able to stay focused on making the system work. I also have to say that I might have enjoyed myself more.

Some nights we would lose, other nights I'd win big and on the odd occasion that we'd made enough in a session, we'd get up and walk before the hour was done. That's called disciplined, scientific blackjack. So at the end of the trip having hit all these casinos, I ended up with twenty-seven thousand, eight hundred dollars. Enough to cover the Vegas marker and enough for me to go out and buy myself a Yz250 Yamaha dirt bike.

! # ⊕ *

THE SABBATH TOUR signified the beginning of the end for our head of security, Big Val. While he was always good at what he was employed by us to do, he started thinking that he was a rock god himself, as did quite a few of the crew by this point. We were always very close with the crew, like one big family most of the time, and when that's the case it's not unusual to have people take advantage of you and rip you off because they start to think they're entitled to what you have.

Vinnie created a lot of these problems because he never did anything about anything. He'd just let things happen. Creating that kind of monster and hating confrontation like he did was a bad combination, particularly when it was obvious that someone had taken things too far like Big Val had. The breaking point came when we found out that he was making his own Pantera t-shirts with our fucking logo on them and planned to sell them front of house at shows. He wasn't a celebrity, he was a fucking security guard, but I guess it's inevitable and halfway acceptable to *think* you're a star when you're in a position like he was. But the line is crossed when a security guy starts using our name for his own monetary gain.

"What the fuck are we going to do about this?" Darrell asked me.

"What fucking choice do we have?" I asked him. "Make up your mind and do whatever you want to do."

So Dime fired him. At least he finally saw sense and made the right call.

CHAPTER 16
SWAN SONG

By the time we went back into Dime's studio to record *Reinventing the Steel* after the Sabbath reunion tour, everyone was pretty well burned out. The excess takes its toll on you and we were all really feeling it. Phil wasn't happy, none of us were actually, and when someone walks in the door with a shit expression on their face it just takes the whole room down. What we really needed was a long time away from each other. Not just a few days or weeks, but a *long* time. You can only work and live that hard for so long before you start to feel it, but everyone else expects you to just put out a happy-go-lucky, good time record. That's not the way it works. Every fucking band runs into that problem, especially the great ones, but ultimately we were four stubborn fuckers, man.

TERRY DATE

I tried to mix *Trendkill* at Dime's place and it just wasn't working, so I had to take it to L.A. to a bigger board to mix it. I was very stressed out. Four records with those guys—almost ten years, that's hard. It's a lot to keep up with. I got to a point where I felt "I don't know if I can do this anymore." Vinnie knew the technology inside out, so it was becoming more a matter of who would make decisions, kind of like a referee. I needed a break at the very least and that's really all there was to it. I got calls all the time throughout the last record because they were still friends and I wanted them to make the best record they could.

———

We all agreed on one thing though, which was that the best way forward for the band would be to create sort of an amalgam of all the best stuff we'd done up until that point and make a record that captured all those best elements. In some ways we wanted to go backwards, but in other ways we didn't.

We wanted to rediscover the creative energy and unity we shared in, let's say, '93 or '94, but we didn't want the record to *sound* as if it belonged there. We wanted it to be fresh and have new energy, and for that reason the finished product sounds a lot different from the previous ones while still being unmistakably Pantera. We were also aware that you can't have the same audience forever. We were all getting wiser and we knew that people grow out of that style of music. So we factored in the fact that our crowd was getting a little older—getting a little bit younger at the other end, too, and tailored our sound to accommodate that. One thing we never did was give in to any trend that may have been out there at the time, and I genuinely believe that's why we had such an insanely loyal fan base. We always stayed true to ourselves and our fans respected that, and instead of getting softer as the money came in we stayed heavy all the way through. I can't think of any other metal bands that were successful with that kind of manifesto.

When it came to producing the record, we'd decided that we were going to do it ourselves without Terry Date. Vinnie had already done the two new studio tracks for the live record, so we knew we could do it. We could probably have been doing it for years, but we always felt as if we needed a safe pair of ears like Terry's to capture us on tape and to keep us grounded and focused on getting the process done.

So as well as it being time for a change of personnel, the fact that we wouldn't have to pay four and a half points and a hundred thousand dollars to the producer was also appealing. Trust me, since we were kids we knew how to make records, so after *Trendkill* it was time to fly the coop because we knew how to capture the sound we made on tape.

We got an astronomical advance to do *Reinventing the Steel*, I can't even remember how much it was, but basically it was all free because we were using our own studio and our own time. You see, record labels are like banks except you don't pay interest. They're contractually obliged to give you half the money up front and the rest when the record is delivered, so we just split it all four ways and did what the fuck we wanted with it. Took the money and ran.

This time we were working with a different type of gear and the whole bit. Had the bass up in the mix a lot more and we just went for a totally different tone. No Terry Date, just Vinnie and Sterling Winfield, the engineer, behind the board, and the sonic results were as streamlined as the payroll.

So we'd get down there with a very focused vision about what we wanted the record to sound like and I know we achieved that. You could say *Reinventing the Steel* was a literal reinvention of sorts because it retained our stamp, and was also a return to the sharper hooks of the past, but it did take a fucking long time to finish.

We'd get three songs done and then we'd take a couple of months off. I'd just had kids and, looking back on it now, that made things a little harder because of the whole light switch deal. I wanted to be in two places at once and that obviously creates conflict, although at that time it wasn't impacting my family life. Not yet, but that was coming.

WALTER O'BRIEN

Trendkill had sold well, yeah, but not as well as the previous two. At the start of *Reinventing*, I wasn't happy either because I was really bummed that the band had been doing this since they were fifteen and now they were in this state of meltdown. I said to them a million times, "Guys, I can always go and get another job. You guys are Pantera. You got your shot and you've got the brass ring, don't throw it away. You were that one in a hundred thousand bands that made it." I felt that there was a possibility that they could be throwing it all away. The reason *Reinventing the Steel* took so long was because Phil wouldn't go to Texas to record. And then it got worse and worse until Phil didn't want to talk to Dime and then Dime got pissed at Phil; then everybody got pissed at everybody else while Kim and I were desperately trying to get them to communicate. Literally we'd call Phil and tell him what Vinnie said and then we'd call Vinnie and tell him what Phil said and so on. We were just trying to get the thing *made.*

Gradually we got the record done, although it dragged on for months because of the disjointed nature of the sessions. Darrell was partying hard as usual, hanging out with everyone he could, whenever he could, all kinds of people, and one of them was the country singer David Allen Coe.

He was from Nashville, Tennessee, too, and they were two of the same even though I'm sure he didn't know what to make of us Texas boys playing heavy metal. Whatever. He must have liked us because he eventually got us to play on one of his own records that came out sometime in 2006.

Darrell called me up one night and said, "Dude, you gotta come and meet this guy." I went over to where they were and he's got his shirt off and stinks like nothing I've ever smelled before. I felt like saying "Dude, take a shower. Deodorant, *anything.*"

He's also covered head to toe in ink, so I stupidly said, "I like that ink man, looks really cool" and no sooner had I said that, he dropped his trousers to reveal the word *Danger* tattooed on his cock, vertically I think, although I didn't look for too long.

Fucking *hell…*

I'm all for ink, got a load of it myself, but who the fuck tattoos their *dick?*

I thought, "I didn't need to see that. That's waaaaaay too much." But Dime thought this guy was the baddest dude ever and they were just perfect for each other, completely over the top, crazy mother-fuckers. In fact I used to think that Dime would have turned out just like him if he was still alive. They were just so similar.

There were lots of other people coming out of the woodwork by now, too—most of them assholes who hung around Dime. They had tattoos of *him* and the whole bit. They'd come up to me and say, "You don't remember me?" To fuck with them. I'd sometimes just say, "Am I supposed to? Did we have a child together?"

"Well, I was on the bus back in …" (fill in the place/time).

"Don't you think there were *other* people on the bus, too?" I'd ask.

Dime and Vinnie seemed to just love having trashy-ass people around them after shows, and I got to the point where I couldn't stand it anymore.

RITA HANEY

As their career moved forward and they became more successful, I wouldn't say that they changed as people, but the people who hung around them *definitely* changed. Some of their best friends had the mentality that said, "Okay, you've made it. You're rich, so that means that you pay for dinner every night and buy all the drinks." I don't think they even realized they were doing it. But if one of

the band guys refused for some reason, all of a sudden
they are the dick! At first, everybody was happy-go-lucky
and they were going places, but that changed as the people
around them changed.

———————

As far as dealing with fans *at* shows was concerned, I'd always sign
all the autographs that I possibly could, and depending on what
mood Phil was in, I'd get him to do the same. It was really important
to me that I made myself available.

I'd go into his dressing room to get him and he'd say, "Man, did
you sign everybody and stuff?," hoping that I'd done enough that he
didn't have to.

I'd say, "Dude, that's part of the gig. You know we've got to do
it."

"All right, let's go and do it," he'd eventually say, and we'd go outside and sign all the kid's shit. That was one way that he and I motivated each other. Even if it was raining outside, you'd have kids who
sat there a long time, all day long sometimes, waiting to get a
glimpse, so the least we could do was get some kind of idea about
what they were doing. See us from their perspective. It felt like the
least I could do. It might be twenty fucking degrees out there and
you still had some kid in a t-shirt waiting to get something signed.
"Please buddy, put a jacket on, you're going to get sick tomorrow,"
I'd tell them. "It's not worth that just to meet us."

I'd put a towel over my head and just get out there even in the
pouring down rain. Of course sometimes Phil just didn't feel like going out. His back hurt too much or he wasn't looking good enough
to go out there—hungover or too drugged out—so I'd sometimes
make the decision for him. But all in all, he at least understood how
much it meant to the kids and we'd both sign until there were no
more kids waiting. We carried that mentality we'd had in the club
scene in Dallas in the early days around with us because we always
tried to hang out with our fans. We'd just sit out in the parking lot,

drinking beer and doing stupid shit with the kids as if we were one of them. Another reason for being there for our fans was that we saw a lot of bands over the years that *didn't* do that.

Obviously it got much harder when things got going on a bigger scale, but our record was getting twenty-five hundred people signed in an hour and a half, and it was our duty to be personable to every last one of them, "Hey man, what's going on? Sorry I can't sit and jam with you but we have to move down the line." I always felt that I had to respect the fans to some degree because they were the ones paying my fucking bills, but it doesn't come down to that completely.

To me the music—or rather their appreciation of it—came first and foremost. Currency—whether it was fifteen or twenty bucks to see the show—was just a piece of paper that said, "I'm here to see the band jam. To live the experience." That's how I viewed the fans, rather than just as someone paying my electric bill. So it was most important to me that we put on a killer show for them.

! # ⊕ *

AROUND THIS TIME, and while we stopped back home on a break, my wife and I moved out of the house that was beside Vinnie, into a bigger house on the golf course at Rolling Hills Country Club. I used the place for socializing with the guys I'd always played golf with over the years. I'd assembled a group of friends, guys who belonged to different associations in town but who all liked to play golf, hang out at the country club, have a few drinks, and the whole bit. What I liked best about this group of guys was that they all saw me as just a normal person.

The money was still really good, so I could still afford to buy things like this big fucking house and a huge grill from Barbecue Galore to sit in an outside kitchen, a big eight-foot-long fucker. I'd buy meat in bulk and keep it in the freezer. When I knew I had a bunch of people coming over, I'd pull one out to defrost on the morning prior. We were always throwing cocktail parties, and I was well known for my secret method of grilling rump roast, kind of a variation on prime rib.

I had a pretty set routine in those days. I'd get up at around ten thirty in the morning, have a couple of bourbons, and then hit the links for the day. I'd grab my golf cart and I was gone. This was my hobby and I played golf religiously, in order to jam the light switch into the off position.

Golf was my getaway, my escape. I just did not want to be around anything to do with the band unless I absolutely had to. Twenty of us played all day long, then it'd be happy hour at Rex's house.

I met some folks who were members at Colonial Country Club, which was the Augusta National of Texas in terms of prestige, and was also the place that my dad and I used to sit and watch on TV, back on the couch in De Leon. My dad never got to play the course but I did. It's an unbelievable golf course—one of the peaches of the South—and I got invited maybe ten times to play in the pro-am at the annual PGA tour event.

ONE OF THE MANY DAYS I was playing at Rolling Hills, I got to the eleventh green and suddenly had a strange sense of spiritual awareness. I just felt something. We were fixin' to stop playing for the day anyway, so I said to the guys, "Look, I have to go." I drove the golf cart in, told my wife, "I'm going to the hospital real quick." I knew something was up. I didn't change clothes, just jumped in my car, and went where I knew I needed to go.

Darrell and Vinnie's mom Carolyn had been diagnosed with lung cancer only a few weeks earlier—which was a shock in itself—and she was being treated in the local hospital in Arlington. She had been like a second mother to me in my teens, and her condition seemed pretty bad. In fact, it was worse than it looked. She passed away ten minutes after I got there. Something or somebody told me that I had to get off the golf course and go down there. Was it God? Who knows, but a voice definitely said, "Get down there and say your goodbyes. She's going."

Obviously the brothers did not take it at all well—they were very close to their mother. Her death really affected them for a long time, long after *Reinventing the Steel*, which finally came out in March 2000 and landed at number 4 on the charts. We liked the album for sure and dedicated it to our fans, but we had no idea it would be our swan song.

CHAPTER 17

THE DOWNFALL!!

You've gotten this far in the book and you probably think I'm some kind of fucking angel. Sure, I'd cracked a few skulls in junior high, ripped off the guys at Fotomat, and rolled a few joints here and there, but that's just what you'd expect from a rock 'n' roller, isn't it? Par for the course, I'd say. But what were we like as people?

It's pretty simple: Phil had had his problems, Vinnie pulled his occasional bullshit, and Dime was just Dime. By 2000 and leading into 2001, the band was hanging by the thinnest of threads and the slightest disturbance could have caused that thread to snap. It was a completely dysfunctional situation that had crept up and bitten us all on the ass.

For me personally—and remember this is my book and a commentary of events from my perspective and mine alone—I didn't really start getting concerned about any aspect of my lifestyle until I had to deal with the consequences of my actions. People have different ideas about what actually constitutes a "consequence," of

187

course—different levels of tolerance and the whole bit—but for me, consequences are things that make you sit up and pay attention because they actually impact your daily life.

It could be related to health, family, the law, or finance, anything that impacts your life in a way that forces you to change your patterns. I always tried to stay away from the law as much as possible throughout my life. In general terms I don't like putting myself in harm's way, and when you break the law, that's basically what you're doing. I never ever felt I was above the law in any form or fashion either, which is something that can easily happen when you're in the public eye.

So up until this point, I didn't really have to deal with any of the consequences of my drinking other than the hangover. I was on the road, living the life, and I never had any problems from the drinking until 2000 (also the year my twin kids were born), when I first noticed that I was having stomach problems, presumably from years of alcohol abuse. I was waking up in the middle of the night—on those nights when I didn't have a mini-bar on hand—with the shakes, the whiskey jitters, the DTs, whatever you want to call them. These symptoms, in my mind, added up to a consequence.

Mentally, alcohol was always on my mind, particularly toward the end of the band, but again, not enough to make me take any extreme measures. But it was creeping up on me. You see, alcohol gradually affects your central nervous system and before you know it, you're at a point where you *have* to have it, even when you're at home and outside the normal confines of your drinking, and that made the whole light switch thing harder and harder for me to turn off and be there for the kids. I could still just about take a day off booze, and as a compromise on some days I tried to not drink until five o'clock. But as they say, it's always five o'clock *somewhere*.

My lifestyle was such that I was used to being up until fucking four in the morning, and that doesn't work when you're at home with very young children. It meant that Belinda and I were living separate lives under the same roof when the kids were babies, and that's when I began to feel *isolated* by my lifestyle—being a dad at home with kids should have been a feeling of pure joy.

The truth is that kids change pretty much everything, including your close friends' perception of you. I've thought about this for a few years now, but I really think that Dime was jealous of the fact that I had kids. I think he felt that they were now my main focus in my life as opposed to him, the band, or whatever, and I don't think he was ever really comfortable with that.

Phil's approach to life was always fairly consistent for half a decade. He was all about extremes in every fucking thing he did. That's how it is with him and it's the extreme that gets him off. If it's sport, he's into boxing. If it's horror films, it's hardcore gore stuff. Black Metal records, Death Metal records, whatever; he's just into the extreme edge of *anything*. In keeping with that type of personality, he also had an extremely sensitive side to him that he never ever presented publicly—other than in his lyrics—and because he and I lived together forever, I had seen it.

Dime, putting aside his obvious musical abilities, was always a character and always gave you a run for your money. He was real witty, very charismatic, and always on the spot. On one hand he usually seemed to choose the right words to speak and on the other he'd sometimes make ridiculous comments because he had no idea *what* to say, and he did both in press conferences. Of course the blinking red light of the camera can make you say things that you wouldn't normally say, so he and I both found it easier to turn into some kind of zombie and shut down rather than opening up. Sometimes journalists would rub us up the wrong way and that just made us want to shut down even more. Thankfully Vinnie was always happy to do the interviews.

In the beginning Vinnie was a good leader because he wasn't as crazy as me and Dime were. He held onto it a little better than we did. He had a weird sense of humor in that he thought he was funny when he wasn't, but he was never the kind of guy who'd sit around telling jokes. When he did make one it was usually the dumbest fucking joke you've ever heard in your life. He did a lot of the business stuff while we partied a lot, but as time passed he got into the partying, too, and we got tour managers to look after all the business.

So we all had our strengths and we had our weaknesses that combined to make Pantera the incredible band that it was. None of us was much worse than the next guy, but the process of living, sleeping, and shitting together two hundred days of the year for fifteen fucking years had really taken its toll by the time it came to tour *Reinventing the Steel.*

Something that may have added to the tension was the fact that we were all pretty intimidating people by nature, so the competition was always on among us. We also wore our emotions on our sleeves, too, and that wasn't helped by the fact that Phil had his "Let's pick on so and so today" mode, and if you were the one that got picked on, the insecurity might hit you.

Then when you throw in all the booze and weed and shit like that, it's no surprise that those merely added to the paranoia—I'm *not* a paranoid kind of person by nature. Things even got physical on occasion. Plenty of times I had to pull Phil off Dime because Dime was drunk, but this kind of thing happens in every band. Four different personalities made up the overall dynamics of the band, and if they'd been the same, it would have been stale, boring dog shit.

So, you can see why we needed a break, but we got the opposite because new tour dates were being added and added. There seemed to be no end in sight. The tour seemed to go on forever. The financial offers were great, but because we felt like we were in a marriage that was going south, that just didn't matter anymore. Something had to give sooner rather than later.

WALTER O'BRIEN

It had gotten to the point that nobody wanted to be around Phil anymore. Nobody. And that started affecting everybody to the point that Rex, Dime, and Vinnie were getting loaded because they didn't want to deal with what's going on, and at one point it looked like we were going to have three buses on the road—which the budget simply wouldn't have supported.

————————

I suppose the writing was on the wall as early as pre-production for the tour. Phil was out of his mind a lot of the time and there were moments in rehearsal where Dime and I would look at each other and say, "Dude, he's singing a different song than we're playing"— that's how bad it got. When we actually got out on the tour, Phil killed it every fucking night, which is typical of him. He rose to the occasion.

We were following Slayer so we had to be spot-on. Phil knew what he had to do. You do not go on after Slayer and not be fucking *gold*. That's one band that you just don't follow if you don't have it. But we had it and it was our show.

There were a bunch of other bands rotating on the bill, too— Morbid Angel and Static-X were two of them—but Slayer was a constant. Dime was real friendly with Kerry, but I never had the closeness that Phil and Dime had with him for some reason. I hung out with Tom more than anybody. He had his chick and his kids with him, but at the same time we'd all hang out every once in a while, get dinner, and shoot the shit. I got to know Tom through Rocky George of Suicidal Tendencies, who was a good friend of his and with whom we'd toured promoting *Cowboys from Hell*.

So while the shows were good, the animosity backstage left something to be desired. Dime was on his own with Vinnie on the bus, and he was starting to hate being around his own brother. I'm sure he grew jealous of me because I'd moved out and no longer had to deal with it. I was in a shit mood most of the time and I found myself jumping down people's throats at the slightest provocation—when I wasn't doing that I drank more and more to numb the ill feeling. Drank *more*.

It got so bad that at one point Dime came to me and said something like, "Dude, how much do you think it would cost to buy my own tour bus?"

I just said, "You're fucking crazy. It'll cost way too much and if you're going to do anything, you'd be better off trying to rent one for the rest of the tour."

But he didn't do that. He just drank more, too, in an attempt to block out all the bullshit.

RITA HANEY

Darrell got to where he was drinking more, almost to the point where he was hiding in a bottle. The issues with Phil were probably in the back of his mind but he didn't realize it at that time. He just felt tired and that if they took a six-month break, everything would be okay. Nobody including him really wanted to face up to what was happening. Darrell would go from town to town hung over saying, "Man, I need a day off to rehydrate" but when he saw kids in the next town standing out there with a bottle of Seagram's saying, "Dude, I've been waiting all year" he just couldn't let somebody down.

———

WHEN WE FINALLY got to the end of the first U.S. part of the *Reinventing the Steel* tour in Orlando, Florida, we did what we always did and threw a big party for the band and all the crew. We'd always get really shit-faced the night before we all went home. It was a Pantera tradition.

Well, on this occasion, we drank all night like always and then went to the airport the next day to fly home. Our production manager Chris Reynolds was the guy dealing with all the tickets and paperwork as we're all standing in line. Well, he was such a mess from the night before that he fell flat on his face in front of the ticket counter. Flat. On. His. Face.

All of us were standing there watching in the first-class line and as soon as the airline staff made the connection that we were all travelling together they said, "Y'all are not getting on this airplane. In fact you're not getting on *any* airplane today."

So me, Dime, and Kat Brooks got Sykes to take us to the nearest fucking private jet place. They had those little jet joints all around the airports so you could just hop onto one of these small Lear jets at great expense. These weren't full-blown *Lears* that you could walk around in; these things were small—had seats in them but no restrooms. We'd sent Katt on a liquor run so that we had something for the flight back to Dallas, and Dime and I got completely hammered for the duration. The only thing was that you obviously couldn't take a piss in these things, so Dime and I just used cups, bottles, or anything else we could get our hands on until we could get off the plane.

At the other end we had limousines waiting for us and they were allowed to drive right up to the plane on the tarmac. We just had to unpack our bags and we were good to go. It was full on rock star living even while the band was imploding around us.

! # ⊕ *

LATER THAT YEAR we played a couple of shows in Japan, came back to the U.S., and then flew out again in September to Dublin for the beginning of the European leg of the *Reinventing* tour, with Slayer as our support again.

Then 9/11 happened.

We were stranded in Ireland, and given what was happening in the world, Dublin didn't seem like the best place to be for a bunch of high-profile Americans. Our hotel was two blocks from the U.S. Embassy and everybody's tension was cranked up to eleven. All we could do was sit and watch British propaganda on *Sky News*, listening to their perspective of what was going on in the U.S., and it was truly frightening. I was in a suite with my living quarters on one side, and a TV room on the other side, and my room became a crew headquarters because I had the case full of booze that we carried around with us.

We had stashes of bottles for days but it was still unclear what was going to happen. On one hand the band guys were thinking that we would be catching a flight home as soon as possible. But on the other, the crew set up the backline at the venue, as if we were going to start pre-production for the tour, because the moment a band does that, they are more likely to get paid by the promoter. Nothing was plugged in, none of the amps or speakers, but by setting it up and showing the will to play, the money is apparently safe.

I got out of the hotel maybe one time in the two weeks we were stuck there because one of the security guys beat up our light guy, so it was my job to take the dude to the fucking hospital and everything. That was another great pain in the ass that I had to deal with.

In my mind there wasn't anywhere that was safe. When you have people flying planes into buildings, anything seemed possible. I have different theories on all that nowadays, but back then I just couldn't believe what I was seeing, so it seemed most secure to just stay in the hotel. Of course Vinnie Paul and Dime wanted to go out every night and I just said, "Y'all are fucking crazy," so again the camps were divided.

WALTER O'BRIEN

They were afraid of travelling around Europe at that time and I can't honestly blame them. If any American band had a big target on their back, then it would be Pantera. Ideally they could have continued the tour—which Slayer did— because it was only America that you couldn't fly into, but they didn't and that's all there is to it. Whether Pantera's reputation in Europe was damaged as a result of bailing on the tour, we'll never know.

————

Eventually we got back home after a week in Dublin. We had to fly over the Arctic Circle and down through Chicago to Dallas.

Pantera never played live again.

There was willingness from me, Darrell, and Vinnie to start getting the next record together. But as I've said before, we all needed a break from Pantera. I preferred to be active in my time off and Phil was of a similar mind, but Darrell and Vinnie weren't doing anything after we got back from Dublin, other than waiting for us to be ready to start working again.

Seeing a good opportunity, I got on the phone with Pepper Keenan in New Orleans and started talking about getting the process for a second Down record off the ground so that at least I was doing *something*. Within a few days we had gear loaded onto a truck in Nashville to be taken down to New Orleans. I then got Kim Zide Davis at Concrete Management to get us a record deal, secure the publishing. By October we started recording in the studio with Warren Riker, the Grammy-winning producer/engineer and an acquaintance of Pepper Keenan.

Phil's main house was across Lake Pontchartrain on seventeen acres of land. He had a big, vacant barn there, and Pepper Keenan was really good at fixing things up. He's one of those guys who wakes up in the morning and will build a fucking birdhouse or something, just for the fuck of it. He's real crafty when it comes to shit like that. So he got a saw, bought planks of wood, some paint, and built a den with a bar in it that we called "*Nod*feratu's Lair." Phil would be nodding out all the time, so that's why we gave it that name; the sign is still sitting there above the bar today.

Phil had built a jam room on one side of his property, and Pepper and I built a control room when we first got in there with the gear. We took a whole wall out, the whole bit, to fit it all in. There was an upstairs apartment that had bunk beds in it, a full kitchen, and a pool table with couches all around. It was the perfect hangout pad. So that's basically where we slept and ate—we had people bringing over food when we weren't cooking on the grill outside. I grilled four or five times a week probably, that's how much I was into it. These guys had never had chicken on a beer can before, a Texas thing that I'd perfected over many years. I'd been doing all this stuff way before it was ever shown on TV.

We'd take it in shifts to record, and we had an engineer there who slept in a tent outside on this little-bitty love seat. It was like a fucking M.A.S.H unit: whoever was up in the morning was good to go. So I ended up playing a lot of the guitar parts on that record as well as all the bass, because these other guys would stay up for two days whereas I went to sleep every night.

Phil doesn't like to record until the fucking sun is down. He's like fucking Dracula in that respect. Some nights he was on and some nights he was fucking fried. Despite that it took us only twenty-eight days to record the record, but they were rough days, I'm telling you. I even had to go to the hospital at one point, and that's when the complications really started to show in my stomach. Things were much worse than they'd been.

I took a break at one point and went back home for two or three days to see the family, and I played all this shit for Dime over at Vinnie's house and he loved it. They were fine about it, but they just didn't know that we were going to tour for a year and neither did I at that point, quite frankly. I didn't really want to either; I just wanted to make a record. Then Down were offered Ozzfest; you just don't pass up shit like that. There was another factor that changed the tour plans: the record blew up when it came out. It was just one of those things. It hit a nerve with the metal community, and if people want to come and see you live, you'd be crazy not to go out there and make the best of it, so you can see how the Down thing just grew and grew.

More important perhaps, I was actually happy for once. Down was something new for me, for the first time in fifteen years. I just considered it to be part of my life, my musical journey if you will. I was actually pretty stoked by what was happening.

RITA HANEY

Darrell was very good at recording things, phone conversations, etc., just like he did visually by carrying a video camera around, so there are conversations where Phil called the house throwing a complete fit, threatening to quit the band if he couldn't release the Down record, and that Darrell and Vince had to call Sylvia at the label to fix it. Darrell called him right back and said, "Relax, what's going on?" and Phil even said then, "I'm not trying to tour much; I just want people to hear my music." Darrell and Vince called the label and said, "Okay, let him put it out. It's not a big deal."

———————

Let me say this though: My perspective was not, "I don't want to be working with Pantera." It was much more a case of "I want to do this Down record" because we'd been talking about this thing since '98 and it was widely discussed between all of us that the thing that Pantera needed most was time apart.

But most of all, as always, I just wanted to jam.

I had no idea how it would all unfold—how much we'd end up touring the Down record and the whole bit—I just knew that I needed to keep myself busy and pay the bills for my family. It was also refreshing, and that was what I needed at the time. One thing I do remember is a telling conversation I had with the president of the record label East/West Elektra, the label we shared with Pantera.

I said to her, "We have one more song on this record that needs to be a single and it would make us very, very happy if you could do us the pleasure of doing this."

Of course I felt like adding, "We've only sold *how* many fucking records for you motherfuckers?" in reference to how many units Pantera had sold for our East/West label. But she said, "Honey baby, it ain't never gonna happen. I just want a new Pantera record out." Her name was Sylvia Rhone, and it was our record sales that had put her on the map in the first place, so all she was concerned about was her quarterly sales report.

To me that said *everything*. She couldn't give me the time of day but she wanted a new Pantera record? This woman didn't care about what was going on within the band. She just wanted her sales figures to look good, and at that point I thought, "Okay, this ain't fucking working."

WALTER O'BRIEN

It probably didn't help Rex's position with the brothers when he went and played with Down. I wasn't exactly thrilled about it myself but I also felt that they should all be able to do what they want, as long as they all kept their eye on the fact that Pantera was the main thing. Rex clearly knew that, Phil clearly didn't. It was Rex's call and I definitely respected that he felt he had to keep working. But I felt that Phil was keeping his best songs for Down while giving Pantera all the loud, obnoxious stuff. Pantera were already the arena band, so I felt like saying to him, "Why not let Pantera go triple platinum and then you can go off and do any kind of hardcore side-projects that you want, but Pantera should always be the goal."

Down II was released at the end of March 2002, and we ended up touring for six or eight months out of that year—as I said, I just hadn't envisioned that at all. Our own tour started in April, led straight into a spot on the Ozzfest cycle, headlining the second stage. This was a major opportunity to increase our growing fan base.

I also didn't expect that for almost the next two years, I'd be completely out of control with the drinking and on the way to petrifying my stomach, turning it to stone. The party never seemed to stop.

At one point we stopped in Vegas for a couple of days on the way to the West Coast, and Pepper and I had a suite laid on by my buddies the Maloof brothers. We were drinking heavily and snorting up half of Peru, so I was completely fried by the time we got to L.A. I had alcohol poisoning, but we still played L.A. I didn't want the whole mess of dealing with that fucking crazy scene. Whenever you go to L.A., every crazy fucker seems to come out of the woodwork looking for something. It's renowned for being home to a lot of music industry hangers on, and that was something I wanted no part of. So instead I passed out and came to my senses the next day when we'd reached San Francisco.

We get to the Fillmore where we were due to play that night, and I'm faced with an impossible situation. There was no booze on the bus.

Nothing. Shaking like a leaf on a tree.

Zero.

And by this point I'm starting to seriously freak out. Desperation sinks in. I'm in one of those "I *gotta* have something" type of modes. I felt totally paranoid, probably because Pepper and I had done so much blow the last couple of days. I had to get myself straight, but there was just nothing there to get fucking straight with. So by the time we get to the side of the stage to sound check, I'm a nervous wreck.

James Hetfield just happened to be there at sound check and we were all like "Hey James, how's it going?" During this time, Hetfield had just gone through nine months of living hell of his own and was brand-new sober. And predictably, Phil and he had a kind of "who's got a bigger dick?" type thing going on—particularly as Phil had said that Metallica were a bunch of pussies onstage at some point previously.

Then Grady our guitar tech said to me, "Rex, I've got a bottle downstairs" and thank fuck someone did. So I went and found it inside one of the stage cases. I tried to take a shot but I was shaking so much I almost poked out my eye with the bottle, and spilled whiskey all over myself. But it composed me and temporarily restored my senses, and we ended up playing a great show.

Now I was *really* starting to feel the consequences of excess. And no wonder. We'd snorted most of South America during that fucking summer and in combination with all the drinking—*waking* up in the morning drinking sometimes—all this shit seemed to be crystalizing in my stomach. That's what happened to Stevie Ray Vaughan apparently. He was allegedly dissolving cocaine into his whiskey, damaging his stomach lining in the process.

The biggest problem was that it now seemed like I was out of control *without* booze. It got to where it took me at least a quarter bottle to get me straight, to take the edge off, otherwise I'd be freaking out while also dealing with all the psychological shit your mind plays on you. I'm damn sure the cocaine didn't help, but the alcohol was my main problem and I think that a lot of my alcohol dependency can be traced back to when relations in Pantera became very stressful. Obviously I drank before, to a level far in excess of the norm, but the reason I became dependent on it to live was almost certainly stress related. The business I was in didn't help either, because if you didn't have a beer or a shot in your hand people thought you were sick. Ironically, I actually *was* sick.

THE 10TH OF DECEMBER 2002 sticks out in my mind. I was lying in bed when I got a call at five or six in the morning. Down were going to Japan and I'm all packed up ready to go. Half the band was coming from New Orleans supposedly, but this call came from Sykes: "Phil's not coming."

So I called Jimmy Bower, Down's drummer, and they were sitting in fucking McDonald's somewhere—the problem seemed to be that they didn't have any dope. They had a twenty-hour flight to Japan and they didn't know what they were going to do. I know what it feels like when you can't get whatever it is that you need, so I understood that, but what made it worse (for them) was that when they did get to Japan, there was no guarantee that they were going to be able to find what they needed for the next seven days, so it was going to be a fucking living hell for everyone.

So Phil just called the whole thing off.

Japan trip cancelled.

He wouldn't even get on the fucking phone, and when he eventually did I could just tell that he was super distraught.

I said to him, "Dude, you're blowing a huge money deal here. We're getting a shitload of money to play this one big-ass festival show."

But they were either just so dope sick or simply couldn't find dope, but for whatever reason, Pepper Keenan just said, "Fuck this, I'm not dealing with you cats ever again." We had to pay the deposit back to the promoter and would probably never get asked back to play in Japan again.

At this point I also told Phil that I was never jamming with him again until he was done with dope. And that wouldn't be for another three years or so.

CHAPTER 18

LOST LOVE AND THIRTY DAYS IN THE HOLE

Obviously the whole Down meltdown was a problem when I returned home. I started having repercussions on that front, because by then I couldn't even find the fucking light switch, far less turn it off. The switch was stuck in the "on" position, and it was bigger than the house. I tried though, and managed to keep a handle on home life most of the time. When my wife was working I had no problem driving the kids to kindergarten or doing whatever was needed to take care of them without having a drink.

The kids went to a Christian school from a very young age because we wanted them to have an early understanding of right and wrong, and it was around this time that I first went to a doctor and said, "Something's not cooking. I'm waking up in the middle of the night, jittery as fuck. I need something to help me." And so that's when he first turned me on to Xanax to help with my anxiety.

Did I get addicted to Xanax, I hear you ask? Lots of people who take it seem to, but with me the answer was no. But I definitely found that it helped with the tension. Belinda was sympathetic to my situation, as far as taking care of the kids and everything else that we needed done was concerned, so that allowed me to just kick back and be myself at that point.

But things gradually got worse. Of course they did.

Xanax only eased the anxiety that my drinking problem created but didn't address the root problem in any way whatsoever. Belinda and I were getting into disagreements a lot of the time, so I decided that the next move was to go into rehab. She wasn't pushing me to do it, not at all. In fact if I'm honest, I went in for her sake—to save my marriage.

I went to Jeff Judd's place one night sometime in 2003, desperate to talk to someone about my problems with alcohol. "I can't live like this anymore," I think I told him. "I feel like I'm killing myself."

"Then do something different," Jeff said.

"Like what?" I asked him.

"Why don't you go into rehab?" he suggested. "What have you got to lose? You feel like shit right now, so how much worse can it be?"

He was right. And if I didn't like it, he and I made a pact that I was going to walk my ass out of there. So we agreed right then that I'd at least go in to see what it was all about, but before I did, Jeff and I sat and got totally hammered with a bottle of Crown Royal. Then I got the phonebook out and found a rehab facility that was literally down the street in Arlington that actually turned out to be a fucking mental health facility.

JEFF JUDD

We sat down there, fucking hammered, and the reception guy came out and put Rex through the whole interview deal, after which he said, "I need to take a breathalyzer sample." So Rex does it and the guy looks at it and says "Hold on just a minute, I'll be right back." I said to Rex, "Dude, you blew the meter right off it!" Then the guy came back with another and he blows into it and the guy looks at it and just shakes his head.

————————

They must have given me some kind of sedative that night so that I didn't have a seizure. When I woke up the next morning, I had to fall in line with all these fruitcakes. I looked around trying to get my bearings, and this girl came up to me who looked like she'd fallen face-first into a fishing tackle box.

"Hi, I'm a cutter," she said, pulling up her sleeve to show me the cuts, and she had twenty-one fucking earrings all over her face.

"Where the fuck *am* I?" I asked somebody.

"Oh, you're at Millwood Mental Institute," they told me. Well, this place was fucking wild. I thought, "This is not rehab, this is a mental institute and I'm not mental."

"I'm discharging myself right this fucking minute. I'm in the wrong fucking spot right now." I went home and did more research, and found out that there were a couple of real facilities around, one of them close to home, so I checked myself into that place the very next day.

I wanted to see what this concept of addiction is all about. I was genuinely interested in the process. I'm curious like that—it dates back to my childhood days of reading endless books—so I wanted the whys, the hows, and the whole fucking bit. Or at least I thought I did. The problem is, once you learn about the ways of addiction and the *waves* of addiction, well, then the party in your fucking head really starts rolling.

All of a sudden you're armed with *too much* knowledge and you use that information you have to try and outwit the problem. Of course the irony is that by doing so you are merely confirming your addictive issues. You can drive yourself fucking crazy thinking about being sober. For example, if I saw someone leave a half-finished beer on the table and walk away, that would really piss me off, probably because they could do it and I knew I never could.

You also lie to yourself. Of course you do. That's part of the process. You convince yourself that you can stop at any time, you think, "I'm in control of this and that" type of shit, but you can't stop anything and, deep down, you know it. It's called denial. Looking back now, I wish I had never gone looking for the information because it completely fucked with my head.

But my first rehab got me healthy on a superficial level at least. I went in for around thirty days, they gave you the right foods to eat. You go to these classes all fucking day long and put up with a bunch of other idiots, fucking people who—while you're there really trying to help yourself—they're on their sixteenth fucking rehab. The way all that works is just retarded, but your head gradually turns and when the thirty days are up, you do feel better. Was it the end of my problems? No, but it was a start and also *the* start of a long process.

JEFF JUDD

He found a place up in Grapevine that was a pretty well-thought of facility, so he went up there, checked himself in for a thirty-day program, and when he came out he functioned amazingly and didn't touch a drink for six months. He was physically healthy and mentally healthy. Everything in his life was kicking ass and all he drank was coffee, coke, and water. I thought he had it licked.

The whole point of rehab is that when you come out, you don't drink. Not an occasional beer or a glass of wine with dinner. Nothing. So what triggers the process of starting to drink again, having gone through thirty days of trying not to? Well, with me, it was something like if my shoes were fucking untied, I'd have a drink. I'm serious. Any fucking thing would give me a reason to jump on the sauce and for the next couple of years I would go back and forth with the business of drinking and trying to quit, simply because I hadn't made the decision to quit—for *me*. I'd made it for every other reason *but* me. The guilt alone will kill you.

My wife and I had discussed the idea of moving out of Texas in 2003, but nothing had happened to make us act on that impulse. Maybe we both needed a change of scenery, who knows, but it was more complicated than you think, because I actually had four properties that I needed to dispose of before we moved anywhere.

2003 WAS ALSO THE YEAR where communication within Pantera was at its most strained. Phil basically dropped off the map completely and wouldn't answer anyone's fucking calls, ours, management's, or anyone else's. I never talked to him but I was caught in the middle of *trying* to talk to him. Instead he went off and did the whole Superjoint Ritual thing and hardly told us he was doing it, and the rift between us got deeper and deeper to the point where I walked past him at a show somewhere and he didn't even recognize me.

WALTER O'BRIEN

After the second Down record, it seemed like Pantera was no longer Phil's priority, and it didn't help that for the three years after *Reinventing the Steel*, Phil wouldn't call anyone back. Not us, not the band, not *anyone,* and it got so bad that the only way to get any answers to anything band related was to pass a message on to one of his friends in New Orleans and they would then have to drive out to his house in the woods to give him it. He couldn't give his

attention because he was going to be in the studio with
Superjoint or on tour with Superjoint, or he was going to
be wherever with whoever.

————————

"Phil and I are just tired of you guys being such fucking assholes.
You think you're being cool to people but you're not."

That's just an example of what I said. Yes, the phone call I made
to Darrell sometime in 2003 is something I wish I'd handled differently. It was one of those late-night-and-loaded type of deals for sure,
but I meant everything that I said in its lengthy duration: how I
couldn't stand all Vinnie's bullshit, and how I needed a break from all
things Pantera for a while. I was tired of strip clubs and all the associated crap that I was dealing with, so when you're caught in the middle for as long as I was, sooner or later the levee's gonna break, and it
finally did, so I had to say what I fucking said.

In the back of my mind there was more to it than that, though.
I'd just had kids and wanted to see them grow, so the time off that I
needed was going to fulfill that purpose also. But in retrospect I think
I confided in the wrong person. I probably should have just told my
wife or someone and vented it that way.

I actually thought at the time that Darrell had taken what I said
all right, but the next time I spoke to him it was obvious that he
hadn't. He called the next day and said, "That was pretty fucking
harsh, man." And I apologized—reminded him I was loaded—and
that again, I just needed a break. But now there was a distance between us that I hadn't felt before.

RITA HANEY

Phil had stopped answering the phone, and Darrell felt like
he'd been stabbed in the back because Phil wasn't doing
what he said he'd do. They arranged a meeting in New
York, but Phil didn't show up and Rex was caught in the

middle of it all. Rex called one night, really intoxicated and it lasted a good three hours. He said some pretty harsh things to Darrell, who was completely sober at the time, and I know they were drunk words but it did seem like there had been some animosity building up and it sounded like he had Philip in his ear, too. I'm sure he regrets a lot of what he said. Darrell was trying to pump Rex for information about what was going on because he couldn't find out anything from anybody else. Phil would not answer the phone and wouldn't say what he was really trying to do and this was when Darrell realized that they were in trouble. Maybe there was no more Pantera. Philip totally has barriers. You can't just pick up the phone and call the dude; you usually have to go through a couple of people so that made it easy for him to shut himself away, especially in his compound, which at that time was still a heroin den.

———————

2003 continued with very little direct band communication at all. I ran into Darrell at a Motörhead show in Dallas a few weeks after that phone call, and he wouldn't even talk to me. I'll never forget the look on his face. I still have it in my mind. It was a *horrible, terrible* look but what could I do? I said what I said and couldn't take it back.

Vinnie and Dime were really hurt by what was happening and at a certain point they just said, "Fuck it, we're going to start another band," as if to say, "Fuck y'all." I didn't understand why that sentiment was directed at me, but when it was, that line was drawn in the sand. I was all for them doing their Damageplan thing, so I just said to Dime, "Do what you've got to do, man." As I've said a million times: I wanted time away from all things Pantera.

! # ⊕ *

I SPENT THE REST of 2003 and early 2004 doing things that had absolutely nothing to do with Pantera.

I was enjoying watching my kids grow and hanging out partying on my thirty-foot powerboat. I bought it back in '98; it had a full kitchen, could sleep six, and was docked up at Grapevine Lake, also known as "Party Lake." We'd go out there—take the kids, too—and one of my best friends was a dock mate, so we'd just say, "Okay, let's go to the lake" and we'd head out there on a Thursday night and party until Sunday. The boat had flames painted on the back. I named it "The Hell Yeah." Vinnie later stole that name for his band.

PERIODICALLY I'D HAVE TO deal with communication from the Abbotts, Vinnie mainly, but all he would ever do was bitch about what Phil was or was not doing, so there was nothing really for me to do or say. Phil still wasn't talking to us, but he was more than happy to discuss his plans with the press. It became obvious as 2003 dragged on that his intentions were different than what he'd initially said.

We were in limbo.

And while I was happy to finally have time to relax and spend time with the family, I had no way of predicting exactly what Phil's longer-term plans were, particularly when he recorded a *second* Superjoint record and started intimating in the press that they were his main focus. I would rather he had talked to us about it.

Phil had a different manager by then, and at one stage of this whole communication vacuum, his manager was calling *me* to get answers about Phil and his new band. I'd just say, "Fuck you, dude."

"Hey man, I'll manage you, too," he'd say.

"What are you going to manage? There's nothing *to* manage," I explained.

"Maybe I could get Pantera back together?"

"Who the fuck do you think you are? You're a fucking douche-bag." His name was Dennis Rider.

What does it say about the state Phil was in when his own manager was coming to me for information?

KATE RICHARDSON (Phil Anselmo's girlfriend)

Superjoint Ritual were out on the Ozzfest tour in 2004 and we had a date in Dallas. Everybody else was being all dramatic saying, "Oh my God, Oh my God, what happens if they meet the brothers?" But Philip and I between us both thought, "Man, I really hope they [the Abbots] do show up." Philip said to me, "I'd want to pull them into a room, give them a hug and say, 'This is all bullshit, I love you guys. No matter what projects we're working on, I love you.'" We were at first told that they never showed up at the show, but we later found that they did show up but people steered us all apart and, between security coordination or whatever, made it impossible for Philip and the Abbott brothers to see each other.

We were now in the middle of a "he said, she said" bullshit thing in the media where Vinnie and Phil took increasingly personal cheap shots at each other in the music press. Darrell stayed out of the conversation mostly, but did allude to Phil's ongoing drug issues in an interview with *Guitar World,* but only after being provoked earlier.

I didn't get involved at all. I said *nothing whatsoever.*

It all seemed so childish to me and I felt that the only way to *really* reconcile would be for us all to be in the same room at the same time. However, Phil was still using, that much we did know, so I suspected that nothing constructive was going to happen until he got clean, and when that time came I was going to be the one who had to bring the two sides together to at least *start* discussing the future. Until all those components fell into place, I had decided that I was going to stay far away from all of playground name-calling.

KIM ZIDE DAVIS (one of Pantera's management team)

My perspective is a little different from everyone else's maybe, because I genuinely was stuck in the middle, particularly near the end. Rex and Philip's take on how things went down is very different from Vinnie and Dime's take, though, I do know that. It really came down to the lack of communication. The separation had gradually happened over the years. They had different interests because they were four different people, and Vinnie and Dime's personal interests were more related to each other, as were Rex and Philip's. So that put the rift right through the middle of the camp. Rex was definitely the peacemaker between Vinnie and Dime and Philip, because he could speak with Philip and Philip would listen, then Rex could take the information back to Vinnie and Dime. Rex was obviously not involved in heroin but neither was he involved enough in Vinnie and Dime's partying, so that detachment made him the obvious mediator, almost by default. That had been his role for a long time because they were always on the road. He was the face-to-face middleman, whereas my contact was mostly on the telephone.

———

From the phone conversations that Darrell and I had on my birthday in 2004, then again in November of that year, it seemed as if we were both at least on the same page regarding what we hoped for in the future. Darrell and I had been friends since we were kids after all, and it seemed that despite how tense our relationship was at that time, neither of us was prepared to let go of the time we'd spent to-gether, which meant something. Yes, there had been hurtful things said, but the reasons for that were more because of the generally tense situation than any personal issues between us. Hand on my heart I believe that.

RITA HANEY

I talked to Rex a couple of times before Darrell talked to Rex on his birthday, and he was trying to find out from me if Darrell had mutual feelings, which he did. So when Rex called, I asked Darrell if he wanted to talk to him and he said he did. Not just that, I think this could have been the start of trying to fix some things and to reach Philip. Darrell was still pretty angry though and didn't want the blame to be focused on Philip. He wanted everyone to take their share of the blame. For all of them to step up. He said to Rex, "You know the only reason I'm talking to you right now is that we have history. You're my brother and you lived on my couch." He still loved Rex, no matter how angry he was with him.

When you boil it down to basics there really was no blame to be leveled at any one individual. We all wanted to be working on *something*, to be making music, so if it was necessary for us all to go our separate ways for a while, so that we could all come back to Pantera refreshed when the time was right, then that seemed like the obvious way forward—and the only way to get back to where we once were.

CHAPTER 19

THE WORST DAY OF MY LIFE

However delicate our relationship was throughout most of 2004, the events of the night of December 8 ensured that we would never know what the end result of the conversations might have been.

KATE RICHARDSON

I was at home and I don't know what Rex and I were talking about, but we were on the phone together when the news about Darrell came in. One of our mutual friends who was a sound guy in the industry called me on another line, and so I told Rex what I was told. We were totally freaked out but we didn't know at this point that it was fatal. We just knew that there had been a shooting and that

Darrell had been shot. So we had to both get off the phone to get *on* the phone with other people in order to find out what was actually going on. What is really strange is that the previous night I'd had a dream about Darrell and in the dream I had to babysit him. It was bizarre. Philip and I always discuss any dreams we have, and when we were lying discussing it the next morning for two hours he lay there talking and reminiscing about Darrell saying, "Fuck all this bullshit. I have got to call that guy. I'm going to call him today." Then people came over to the house and he never got the chance to make the phone call before we got the terrible phone call.

———

WALTER O'BRIEN

The lease on my office in Manhattan expired in 2003 and I knew then that my career in management was probably over so I went back to college to get my Bachelor's Degree in Journalism at Rutgers. At the end of 2004 I was almost in the last semester and had important mid-term exams. I was out having dinner with a bunch of friends, sort of mourning the [anniversary of the] passing of John Lennon, and then I started getting phone calls from everyone telling me about Darrell.

———

I've said already that what happened that night not only shook me profoundly, but it also left an indelible imprint on every second of my life since then. Band tension created by years of close quarters living is one thing; the loss of life, particularly when that life belonged to one of the people dearest to me on this planet, is entirely another. In an instant, all the petty bullshit that had plagued us the previous few years seemed completely meaningless.

KIM ZIDE DAVIS

I got a call at around 10:16 p.m., which was roughly two minutes after it happened, and I was told that there was a shooting at a Damageplan show, and that Dime was definitely dead but they weren't sure about Vinnie's status or anything else at that point. I was in a state of total shock, so I can only rely on what my husband tells me, and that is that I sat on the couch and the phone didn't stop ringing until about one in the morning, at which point he took my phone away from me, turned it off, and put me in bed. The details are all fuzzy. On the day of the funeral, I remember getting to Texas and going to the hotel where they had set up everything. It was really surreal because friends from all over the world were there, people we used to see, other musicians and people from the music industry who we didn't ever see in Texas, far less all together in the same building. Everyone was in the same state of wondering, "How could this have happened to Dime?"

———

A more immediate concern was the fact that the line that seemed to have been drawn in the sand between the band members meant that the funeral was going to be awkward territory, especially as far as Vinnie and I were concerned.

For me it was that fear of the unknown—I just didn't know how Vinnie was feeling because we simply hadn't been communicating. As it turned out, the messages I was receiving were mixed at best. Obviously Vinnie was distraught about what had happened—we all were—but there was that contradictory aspect to how he viewed me that he just couldn't hide, despite his sadness.

He wanted me there, but he also felt I was in some way to blame for his brother's death. Go figure. I really didn't know where I stood, and if *I* didn't know, Phil would have had no clue whatsoever about where he figured in the overall equation. I know Phil was flabber-gasted by Rita's threats about what she'd do if he came to Texas, but at the same time he was also very respectful of her wishes. However, we all knew where he was habit-wise, so for him to just show up would have been a terrible move.

Looking back on it I feel bad that he never got any closure. Yeah, that really sucks. Being completely excluded and then having to sit there and not be able to talk to anybody must have been very frustrating, and that feeling must have only been heightened when his letters to Vinnie were completely ignored. To date, as far as I am aware, there has been no attempt by Vinnie to make contact with Phil since 2004.

The source of Vinnie's bitterness was an interview that Philip did with *Metal Hammer* sometime in late 2004. Phil's exact comments were that Dime "deserved to be beaten severely," and it was that comment that led to the public's assumption that this was the catalyst that led to Darrell's shooting. Phil said that the comments were fabricated, or at the very least taken out of context, but I have heard the tape recordings and I know what was said.

But, if you're asking me whether I feel that there's a direct connection between the statement and Darrell's death, I would have to say no way. You can't speculate about the mind of a killer. And Phil was in no way to blame for what happened that night. The press just seized hold of his words and spun them to suit their own narrative goals. To me it was just a case of ill-chosen words combined with really unfortunate timing. But that's no consolation to Darrell or those close to him. Knowing what Darrell was like, the only possible consolation for him was that he was buried with Eddie Van Halen's guitar by his side in a KISS casket. Terry Glaze said at the funeral that if we'd told Darrell that he'd be buried with Eddie's striped Kramer off the cover of *Van Halen* when he was seventeen, he would have probably said, "Okay, kill me now."

RITA HANEY

I convinced Vinnie to let Rex come to the funeral. Rex
showed up at my house before Vinnie even got home from
Columbus, and I was mad at him but I just took one look
at him and started sobbing, hugging, and crying. It wasn't
about those little petty issues anymore. Then I remember
when Vince got home I told him Rex had come over and
he was really mad. I said, "Darrell would want him here."
And I told him that Rex and Darrell had talked on the
phone and so I convinced Vince that I wanted Rex to be
one of the pall-bearers. Vinnie was resistant at first but
then he said, "You know what, if that's what you think,
and that you think that's right, then okay." I voiced that
I thought everyone should have the right to say their
goodbyes to Darrell even if it was at separate times,
because nobody wanted to see Philip, but Vinnie was
dead set against that. He let me make the call on Rex, so I
couldn't deny letting him make the call for Philip. I didn't
completely agree with it, but what sold me on it was that
for Philip to show up drugged out would have been so
disrespectful and I had already heard that he was in a
hotel room in exactly that state.

————

KATE RICHARDSON

We didn't get on the phone with Rita until the day after
Darrell's death, and at that time Rita was telling Philip not
to come. But we felt "How are we not going to come?" So
we went ahead and went to Dallas, but that's as far as we
could go. We didn't want to upset the family, but at the
same time we felt that this was the time for everyone to

have closure. In Philip's mind this transcended all the miscommunication that had gone on over the previous months. When Rita was on the phone with Philip, she was telling him not to come, but at the same time other people are picking the phone up saying, "Why the fuck are you not here? You should be here right now." And all Philip could say was, "Well, if the lady of the house doesn't want me there, who the fuck are you to tell me to be there?"

———————

The funeral itself and the days that followed it were some of the most emotional days of my life and it's hard to remember one moment from the next. It was almost as if I wasn't really there at all but was merely looking in on the scene from somewhere else, but one thing I knew was that the pain I felt at the loss of my best friend was real. I was deeply upset, but I was also feeling two other emotions. The first was a real and growing fucking hatred for the guy who had done this to my brother, and the second was the constant, unanswered question of why this happened. I badly wanted to find out, but there were no obvious answers.

KIM ZIDE DAVIS

Rex was like I have never, ever seen him before. Physically he was standing there, but that's all. Literally like he was on another planet. It was as if he had no way of grasping that what was happening was real, and I couldn't really blame him in a lot of ways. I barely made it through myself, and I had just been Dime's manager. I hadn't been in a band with him for twenty-something years. I didn't notice any inappropriate behavior on the day, probably because there was always crazy stuff going around the band and Darrell was the king of that, but a lot of people had been drinking heavily and when they eventually

helped Rex out of the memorial service, it was clear that
he was inebriated.

———————

KATE RICHARDSON

This was all a really insane, fucking crazy time. Philip and
I were both asked to not go to the funeral, but we went to
Dallas anyway and were just waiting for approval to go
to the funeral itself. We were planning on going but then
people were starting to make death threats to get us to stay
away. But we were in Dallas for a week staying in a hotel,
and during that time we went over to Rex's rental house
and we spent a bit of time with him before the actual
funeral. We didn't go to Darrell and Rita's house; we drove
past a few times but didn't dare go to the door. Rex was
very confused and angry when he saw Philip, as everyone
was. We wrote letters to Vinnie while we were staying in
the hotel, and as far as I understand he has never actually
opened them and the report back was that he had no
intention of ever doing so.

———————

BELINDA BROWN (Rex's ex-wife)

I don't think Rex was stable enough to make any decisions
around the time of the funeral. For some of the guys their
way of dealing with the grief and the loss was to all get
together and start pouring shots to celebrate a life, so
when people like Eddie Van Halen and Zakk Wylde had
to do the official part of their duty at the funeral, they
were hardly able to speak because they were so drunk,
and it turned into the Zakk and Eddie show.

———————

WALTER O'BRIEN

I wasn't at the funeral. I kept begging Guy Sykes to let me
know what the plans were because I knew I had these
exams to take. I didn't hear anything, and then on the
Sunday, Kim called me and said, "Are you coming?"
"Coming when?" I asked her and she said, "It's tomorrow
morning." I just couldn't get out of these exams, so I just
couldn't go and I've never stopped feeling bad about that.
I spoke to Rex and he even said, "Listen man. We'd all love
you to be here, it would certainly be good for you to be
here, but honestly, you've got to think about your future
and we are your past." And that was pretty damn generous
of him to say that. I've always kicked myself, but I had no
choice.

———

Actually, I was pissed for years at Walter for not showing up for
the funeral, as were lots of other people. He was a huge part of the
Pantera family after all. Walter and I have reconciled recently, but it
still pisses me off.

CHAPTER 20
THE AFTERMATH

Life got harder after Darrell's death, there's no doubt about that. I thought about him all the time and still think about him every single day and, even if my words here have been critical, I do have a lot of empathy for his brother. I need to say that. Life is a far less wonderful place without Dime in my life, and he was my best friend, for years, until we became estranged by circumstances. But that will never change how I feel about him as a human being.

As I said before, my wife Belinda and I had talked about getting out of Texas even prior to that awful night, so we made plans to move to Los Angeles, probably the dumbest place to get away to in retrospect, but I always have this burning desire to keep jamming. Public attention was already high, but after December 2004 it all became too much, and if you've read this far you know how I feel about keeping a low profile whenever possible.

Now I couldn't even leave my house, which had also been broken into while my children and wife were inside the house. She had to scream at the top of her lungs in Spanish to tell this Mexican dude to get the fuck out. I woke up to see this guy standing there with a shotgun under his trench-coat—right in front of my big screen TV, and because it was such an old, well-soundproofed house, we hadn't even heard this fucker get in. Scary shit.

We couldn't even go to the fucking grocery store without being reminded of everything that had happened, as if it wasn't already at the forefront of my mind.

My brother was gone and nothing would ever be the same. Not for me, not for any of us, but for me personally, his tragic death would merely signal the beginning of the incessant question: Why? *Why?*

I spoke to the police in Columbus sometime afterwards and got some kind of insight. From what they said the events of December 8, 2004, weren't necessarily specifically directed toward Darrell. He was just unlucky in the sense that it was his band that happened to be there on the night this guy's rage peaked. The police even went as far as to say that it could have been *any* of us—me, Phil, Vinnie, or Darrell—that got killed if we'd been there. This deranged anger was directed at *all* of us in Pantera.

Now, I don't want to give the fucker that shot Darrell any more coverage than he deserves (which is none whatsoever), so I'll leave alone any further thoughts and opinions I might have. This guy was a fucking nutcase. But what I will say is that the metal press did not help the situation in the months leading up to Darrell's death. Dealing with band issues was our business and our business only, and while fans probably wanted some idea of what our plans were, to have it all play out blow by blow within fucking magazines and on fucking sites like Blabbermouth was not in any way helpful. These were real people and real fucking lives they were dealing with, not some heavy metal reality show for people's daily entertainment. Let's just leave it at that.

! # ⊕ *

AT THIS POINT I was thinking about putting a band together with my buddy Snake from Skid Row. He'd just started working for Doc McGhee's management company, and I had known Doc for years since our days on the road with KISS, who he also managed. Whenever Gene Simmons was in Dallas he'd call me up and ask if I could fix him up at the Clubhouse. One night he called the house and left a message on the voicemail when Belinda was there, and when she told me she said, "Who's Gene Simmons?" "That's Gene Simmons from KISS!" I told her, and I still have his message. "Hey Rex, this is Gene. I know you have the hottest club in town and I want to partake of your party girls."

While there were options to work on something new with Snake, one thing I didn't expect was that Hurricane Katrina would reunite me with Phil Anselmo. Katrina hit in August of 2005, and when it did, it washed pretty much all the dope out of town. It was done. People were looting all the stores and shit, so if you were an addict, chances are your dealer didn't have any drugs to sell you, because nothing could get in or out of the city for weeks. So you could say Phil got off dope by default and thank God he did, and when he says that he got clean, it's true, but mainly because there were no drugs to be had.

I couldn't get in touch with anyone for a month. I didn't know who had made it out and who hadn't. I don't think anyone who wasn't connected in some way to New Orleans even knew that. It was like a different world down there and was a genuinely scary situation. I couldn't get ahold of Phil for three or four weeks, and the only person I made contact with was Kirk Windstein because he'd texted me (the only method of communication that was working) and told me that he was staying at his grandmother's place on the outskirts of the city. It turned out that Phil's house in town was completely ruined—the water came up right over his garage, so he lost most of what he had down below because it was built on stilts.

Vinnie Paul had called me a couple of days before Phil had and he asked me in general terms, "What are you doing?" And I told him,

OFFICIAL TRUTH, 101 PROOF

"I'm just here in L.A. trying to get a gig," which was entirely true at that time.

Vinnie wasn't doing *anything* after his brother died, but since then he and I had at least been on speaking terms. Then as I said, I get a phone call from Phil two days later and he's crying, saying, "Man, I fucked up. I've really seen the error of my ways and I want to clarify that I am not on dope anymore, and that I really want you in my life again." While I knew in my own head that Phil probably had no clue what he had done for the preceding ten years, crushing various people's lives mainly, at this point I believed what he was saying and decided to take him back into my life.

He didn't beg at all. That's not his style; he assumed that I'd take him back, but I told him in no uncertain terms that I wasn't putting up with any of his shit if I did. It gave me comfort that his personality had changed since he had gotten himself clean, though. It took him a while, but he was back to what he does, in that it's all about him. Everything was *always* about him, and soon it was as if the previous few years of hell had never even happened.

"I'm the King of Metal!" he liked to say.

"Well, if you didn't have anyone beside you helping you, you were just another piece of shit." That's my opinion; Kate Richardson was with him throughout his battles with dope, and it's no exaggeration to say that she's the reason he's still alive.

Anyway, when I told Vinnie all this, and that because of it I was considering working with Phil again, his first response was simply "I can't believe you're doing this."

Then he called two or three times over the next couple of days saying things like, "Are you out of your fucking mind?"

"Dude, what are my choices here?" I asked him. "I can do all these soundtracks and try and get my foot in the door on this end, or go back and jam with Phil and deal with the twenty percent brilliance/eighty percent nonsense equation." Next I told him that I had opted for the latter, which included the decision to start writing another

Down record, for which I organized all the management, booking agents, accounting—the whole grid.

RITA HANEY

Vinnie is a very stubborn person and he's never changed ever since I've known him. Darrell had a term that he liked to use to describe him, and that was "Crystal Ball," and it means that he believes in looking into a crystal ball and predicting what he believes to be the future and once you see it that way, that's how you see it, whether it's the facts or not. Vince was that kind of person.

———————

Vinnie just didn't get it at all. At this point it seemed that there was no possibility of Phil and Vinnie ever talking again, so you could say that this point in time signified the true end of the part of my life that was Pantera. There was nothing else to say to Vinnie because the path of my musical journey seemed to point toward being reunited with Phil; my life has always been about the music. I wasn't being cold or in any way unsympathetic to Vinnie's situation, not at all. I just knew that Pantera was no longer possible, not in indefinite hiatus like it had been, and I had to keep living my own life. I also felt incredibly lucky that I'd even had the opportunity to be in a band like Pantera—some people never get one chance—and now I was getting to live the dream all over again with Down. Who gets *two* chances like that?

CHAPTER 21

THE HOLLYWOOD EXPERIMENT

In the wider context of my life, there was another reason for getting out of Texas to see what L.A. had to offer. Warren Riker and I had started our own production company called PopKnot Productions, and he had a great place with a studio over near Burbank and was always having bands in there. I'd go over there all the time, and that kept my focuses firmly on the music.

We produced bands, did movie soundtracks, the whole bit, and it was the *ideal* place to record music. I wasn't making much money from it yet, but we were at least starting to get our foot in the door as a little production partnership. I just wanted to get my head into something else anyway, and because Warren seemed to be having some success in L.A., it kind of made sense for me to see if I could achieve that, too.

Before we left Dallas, Kirk Windstein told me he wanted to do a new Crowbar record, so I said, "Fuck, let me produce it." I wanted to try and get into that whole new realm of steering a project's production, and I wanted Warren Riker to engineer it for me. In the end Warren wanted to take producer credit for it, but it was actually the other way around and I footed the bill for some of the costs.

So we went to a house in the uptown region of New Orleans, with a studio where we had recording gear, and did the tracks fairly quickly. I wrote roughly half of the songs and played a lot of good bass on it, too. We were living in that place while we were recording and we were also using coke at the time. I remember lines of it on the top of the grand piano we used for one of the acoustic numbers, as I was writing a lot on the piano at that time. *Lifesblood for the Downtrodden* was not only one of Crowbar's best records, it was also the start of my trying to get into record production in partnership with Warren Riker.

I had been feeling isolated in Texas for some time, so I wanted to do something else while still being around the kids, to catch up for all these years when I'd been out on the road. So when we eventually moved to L.A. in the summer of 2004, we bought a big, family house out in Porter Ranch. It was a really expensive part of town and a new start.

At some point fairly soon after we moved, me and my buddy Snake Sabo from Skid Row rented a Lear jet with a buddy to fly to Vegas for the night, a less-than-an-hour flight East. Now, I hate scoring drugs. To me it's the most pathetic, sleazy thing you can ever do. It's terrible. I never got into that. If I went over to somebody's house and they had some, of course I did it, but I never actually *paid* for drugs in my entire life.

So the following day back in L.A. after a mad night taking blow, I woke up and noticed that we still had vodka left, so I sat there and drank probably half a fucking bottle. I was completely out of control, and the effects of the previous night's activities were wearing on me so heavily, yet I somehow drove my car over to Jerry Cantrell's house in Studio City just over Laurel Canyon.

I pleaded with him, saying, "Dude, I've got to do something. I can't do this. This is wrong." I had a vial of coke in my boot—fine Peruvian flakes to be precise—and at this point Jerry's a year or so sober, so when I pulled the vial out, his eyes flashed wide open. He was *that* close to using, but I said to him, "Let's flush this shit now. Let's not hang onto it."

He suggested that I go to a rehab place that he knew in Pasadena run by the Mongols motorbike gang. These guys are wild and constantly battling with the Hells Angels, but as a rehab facility it turned out to be a complete joke. The head guy was a prominent figure in the rehabilitation business and they had James Caan's brother in there working as a counselor, which helped attract celebrities in need of drug and alcohol treatment.

In reality it was actually more of a boot camp or a commune than anything else, with most of the guidance coming from gang members. It was sleeping on bunks, four guys to a room sharing a bathroom, just crazy, and for about half the time I was there they had me on Rohypnol anyway.

Why did they have me on Rohypnol?

Well, I forgot to mention that I'd been taking Klonopin as an alternative to Xanax for a while because it's a milder form of anti-anxiety medicine. But the problem with Klonopin is that when you come off it, it's truly a scary thing. You can lose it—seizures and shit—so they put me on Rohypnol and slowly weaned me down. For the last little bit I went to a halfway house where I stayed for another month or so. I'd get up in the morning and just go home for a while. Belinda was at work, so I'd just go home and play computer games and then leave, but I soon realized that, once again, I was seeking rehab for all the wrong reasons.

This time I had been doing it for my family, because they thought I needed help. That won't work. You have to want it for yourself, and at this point that wasn't my primary motivation. but at least I was sober. The thing is: sober and *dry* are totally different things.

Then Belinda and I separated. I suppose it had been coming for a while.

She really missed her friends from Texas and didn't really enjoy L.A, because I was always out trying to make things happen on a business level. Her response to a lot of situations was to just split, and that's what happened here. Obviously when we parted I had to keep paying her mortgage. She was, after all, the mother of my children, and while we could no longer exist compatibly under the same roof, I always wanted to make sure she and the kids were taken care of. Meanwhile, I was going to have to find a place to rent, at least in the short term.

I knew I definitely *didn't* want to move into Beverly Hills because—while it may have been the expected thing to do for a rock star—it was seriously expensive and a world of craziness. So Warren Riker and I decided to move into a house together that we found in Sherman Oaks. Warren's old man had died from alcohol, and he was therefore in a good position to keep an eye on what I was doing, so on a lot of levels it made sense. Although him being from Jersey and me being from Texas inevitably led to a few big spats.

We were living in a very private, gated community and the house itself had two separate living rooms: mine was the Texas side and Warren's was the New Jersey side, and we each had them decorated appropriately. We both remodeled our areas. I put wood floors down, and made it mine.

Now, one thing that comes with addiction is the need to go out and rustle up chicks, and now that I was newly single, our place soon became fucking chick central. And only a certain, very high quality chick at that. These women had to be up to a certain caliber and that wasn't hard at all.

I'd still see the kids on the weekends and I was able to not drink at all when they were with me, but when they weren't around I'd drink in my room because I knew that Warren wasn't going to approve.

Secretive drinking is of course a familiar trait associated with addiction. Drinking in private, hiding bottles in places that even you forget where you've hid them, that kind of routine. Of course, to the person doing it, it's no big deal because you can stop at any time.

Only you don't.

Or if you do, it's for a very short time until—like I said before in my case—the laces of my tennis shoes were untied.

! # ⊕ *

GRADUALLY THROUGHOUT 2006 and early 2007, Down started becoming a significant part of my life and it looked like a new record was possible. Remember, we'd gone out in 2005 with no fucking product—only t-shirts—and sold out every single night of a twenty-one date tour. We definitely knew how to make the band a success.

We were starting to get reaccustomed to each other as people, too, and I would go down to New Orleans to hang out. Everything was written in Phil's barn again and then we moved the whole process to L.A.—band-members and families included—to record *Down III* in various places in town. We did the drums at Sunset Sound and then got a call from Heaven & Hell to play some Canadian dates. Around halfway through the recording process we had a Friday through Sunday off, and so I decided that I'd take Belinda to Malibu.

We hadn't been getting along, and even though we were technically separated, I always loved this place called Paradise Cove, and saw this as an opportunity to spend some time with her to see if we could repair the damage to our relationship.

So I went and found a little hotel there next to Zuma Beach that wasn't too far from Paradise Cove.

In the past we'd taken the kids down there and had a great time, but on this occasion Belinda and I drank entirely too much and things got out of hand. The police were called and the long and short of the story is that they took me to fucking jail at the Twin Towers in L.A., the craziest fucking place you could possibly go to jail at. Just the holding cells alone can accommodate thousands of people; you can get lost in there.

I remember sitting there with my hoodie on, pulled tight down over my eyes because these people were so crazy I didn't want to catch any fucker's eye. Some dude got his nose spread across his face, just because he wouldn't give another guy his sandwich. This was one of the most frightening experiences of my life. Not just that, I obviously couldn't get access to any fucking booze or the pain pills that helped me to recover from the damage that booze had caused, so on all fronts it was a fucking nightmarish experience.

When I finally got out, I took a cab from downtown L.A. to my place in Studio City, and when I arrived the whole band was there in various stages of fucked-upness. I had around two thousand dollars' worth of pain pills in the house because my stomach was really out of control, and Jimmy Bower had been taking them. Phil was out of his mind on something, and Pepper and Kirk were on blow, but they all decided that they were going to stage an intervention on *me* because they had found the stash of booze that I had hidden under the bed. They all wanted me to go into rehab, but they were missing the point on two counts: just because you relapse doesn't mean you have to go into rehab every time, and also it wasn't as if any of these guys could look at *themselves* in the fucking mirror with any confidence and say that they didn't have problems that were at least comparable to mine. To me it was totally fucking hypocritical. Here's these guys getting fucked up in my house, but I'm the one getting singled out for intervention. No wonder I eventually quit the band in 2011, but there were other reasons for that, too.

My main problem at this point was that I was about to have seizures from alcohol withdrawal while I was in jail and that I also hadn't taken any medication for at least forty-eight hours. These junkies sit there and say, "Oh, you're doing it wrong, man. You have to climb the walls and get through it."

"Nope, you're wrong again," I said. You can't just "get through it." There's a physical reason *not* to do that because you can actually die from alcoholic seizure, so I took two of each of the pain pills I had and washed it down with the half bottle of vodka that these guys hadn't found in my house. If I'd waited another three or four hours, I'm not sure I'd be alive today.

I needed to get myself straight again before we went out and toured the record, and this time I did it for one reason and one reason only: for me, Rex Brown. I checked myself into a detox place in Tarzana. In all honesty I knew better than anyone that I needed to go into rehab again, but I certainly didn't relish the prospect of the detox process because that is always the worst part. It was my friend Steve Gibb that suggested this place as the best possible detox option for me.

By the way, Steve is Barry Gibb's (of the Bee Gees) son, and he was his dad's guitar tech for a couple of years before going on to do his own music thing, playing bass in Zakk Wylde's Black Label Society for a while in 2000 and then guitar on Crowbar's *Lifesblood for the Downtrodden,* a record I was involved with. I'd put Steve into rehab at a place called Promises on his own father's request, and now I was asking him to return the favor. Problem was, there were no fucking beds available at Promises, so I had to find an alternative to get started with the detox process.

So Steve recommended this other place in Tarzana and it was fucking nuts going through the detox process there, because in order to do it they had to put me on methadone, which is no fun at all, trust me. You're basically there until you wake up and when you eventually do, you soon realize that you've got another fucking problem: they need to detox you twice. Throughout the whole time I was in there I was calling Steve and saying, "Dude, get me the fuck out of here and get me checked into Promises. There's no way I'm staying here."

Promises is commonly regarded as one of the best rehab programs in the entire country, and it's been used, often successfully, by every musician or movie star you can think of. There are secluded, private locations in Malibu and Mar Vista, as well as an outpatient re-hab center in downtown L.A. It's seriously expensive, as you can probably imagine, but their success rate was apparently very high, so I had it in my mind that they could put me through the whole detox process there, as well as doing anything else that they needed to do.

I was in there for twenty-eight days, and Promises was the answer for me because it was the right program at a time in my life where I was really willing to commit to the process for my future well-being and not for any other reason. That's the key to rehabilitation. Any other agenda only results in a waste of time and money where you end up like Ozzy, who's been to so many rehabs over the years. The story goes that he walked into Betty Ford the first time and they told him, "We're going to teach you how to drink properly," to which he replied, "Okay, so where's the bar?"

"We don't have a bar, that's not part of this deal." Until you get the message that rehab is intended to stop you from drinking, it'll be a long road.

Promises rattled my whole soul, and that's not overstating it at all. The whole program was just insane. As well as a structured series of seminars, they'd also take us out to the Self-Realization Fellowship in Pacific Palisades—and this place was nothing but ponds and flow-ers, complete serenity, and that helped me tremendously. Then we'd go to Topanga Canyon near Malibu to do therapy and spend the day dealing with horses. You're sitting there on a horse with this whip in your hand but you're not whipping the horse; then depending on your body language you could make the horse go in any direction you wanted it to go. The first guy to try it got just nibbled to shit. Horses have a sense about people. In Texas, that's called horse sense.

When I came out of rehab in 2007, Belinda and I (we were still separated at this time) had some pretty severe talks about life in gen-eral. As I said before, she wanted to move back to Texas—she couldn't hang out West—and I was also at the point where I felt like I had outgrown L.A. My social life wasn't the kind that really suited me. We'd go to all these clubs and hang out and that just wasn't me, and there was a danger of me finding myself in a similar situation that I'd left back in Texas a couple of years earlier. I just was not comfortable standing there in celebrity-ridden clubs.

After a lot of discussion and a little time, Belinda and I started getting our relationship back together. You always think the grass is greener on the other side, but she came back around and the truth of the matter is that I was still in love with her. It was as simple as that.

So we moved back to Texas in August of 2007. I got my moving guys to collect all my stuff and put it in storage in a huge warehouse they had for which they only charged me seventy-five bucks a month, and then Belinda and I moved into a little-bitty apartment because I was on the road with Down pretty soon after we got back. Now that I was sober and taking care of business, the tension within Down had eased significantly, and they also must have known that to kick me out of the band would have harmed ticket sales for the tour.

Soon Belinda and I decided to get a bigger place, and because the money was still coming in pretty good, we bought a large house in Colleyville. I had come full circle. *Down III* came out a month after we moved and got great fucking reviews and started selling substantial numbers on the back of that. It was a good record, but I like *Down II* better. I had an attachment to *Down II* that I didn't have with this one because I'd done all my homework on it, got all the gear moved down from Nashville, and the whole bit, and for that reason I take a certain pride in it.

While *Down II* was a great piece of music drawing from a bewildering array of influences, and a record that I had considerable personal investment in, its successor's main strength and depth lay in its message. For all of us involved, *Down III—Over the Under* was about overcoming a whole lot of negative things that engulf us: personal tragedy, addiction, and Katrina being three of the most obvious. Sometimes you can't control these things and so you're faced with a dilemma: be angry and bitter, or take control and just get over it. We chose the latter. We wanted to put out a positive message to show that tough times could make us stronger.

"On March the Saints" was the pivotal song on the record and the kind of song you'd want ten of on any record you ever make. It was focused and direct right from the point where Kirk Windstein came up with the riff and I added the bass line. Then Philip added vocals over the top and we had this monster hard rock song that celebrated the resilience of New Orleans in the wake of natural disaster.

While Pantera's bloodline was still intact because of the fact that two of its members were in Down, both Phil and I viewed Down as something completely separate, perhaps even more than it was when we'd started it as a side project back in '98. While we understood that fans might also hope to see something of Pantera in us, that was something we tried to distance ourselves from. We both went through a lot after Darrell's death—in different ways, too—and I personally felt that my musical journey had to keep moving forward, but still maintain a healthy amount of respect for the past.

WE HIT THE ROAD with Metallica in 2008 as support on their World Magnetic Tour and that whole experience was significant for me for a few reasons. I'd just been through rehab and I know for a fact that James Hetfield went through hell while he was trying to address his problems. Pepper Keenan is one of James's best friends, so he knows exactly how strong James had to be to deal with his issues.

There are two James's that I know and they run kind of parallel to each other. There's the one that kind of doesn't say a whole lot but when he walks in a room there's a presence that makes you shut up. Then there's a side to him that you only see when you sit down with him one on one, which I got the opportunity to do when we were on the road together.

James and I became close because we're in the same kind of fraternity, if that makes sense. I'm an alcoholic and he shared some of my issues, so we'd sit and talk and I got to know a completely new side of him. We'd talk every night about certain stuff—it didn't have to be about recovery—but we continually bonded. We talked about the spiritual aspect of dealing with the kind of lifestyle that we've both endured and he became crucial to me being healthy. He'd be on a jet somewhere while we'd be riding eighteen hours on a bus to get to the show, but he and I would text each other back and forth to maintain the new friendship we'd created. I'd sit and watch Metallica every night from the same spot at the side of the stage, and at the same point in "For Whom the Bell Tolls" he'd come over and hit my hand and I'd stand there thinking, "This is the guy that I met over twenty years ago in Dallas and now they've sold a hundred million records." I couldn't believe that they had come full circle like this.

While Pantera were on top of the world in mid- to late '90s, Metallica were the band that everyone missed while they were doing all the *Load* and *Reload* stuff, and James himself had gone from being really distant and someone I really didn't know to someone who was open and caring toward me. I was always respectful of him when I was around him and that's something that a lot of people forget about. When someone's geared up and about to get onstage in front of twenty thousand people, they need that kind of respect to allow them to go ahead and do their job. It can't be party, party all the time.

Despite being a control fucking freak, James is a very, very knowledgeable, down-to-earth person. He's been in control from the very start despite Lars being the spokesman. You've seen the movie *Some Kind of Monster*? Well, what happened to Metallica was not dissimilar to what happened in Pantera, in that the tensions were caused by years of living, breathing, and shitting together. You could say that James had problems when that film was shot, but they *all* had fucking problems for the same reasons that we had. And as I learned finally, it doesn't get any happier until you get yourself into a place where you make the connection between your health and your happiness. If you take care of mind, body and soul, everything else that comes is just a blessing.

After you've been through all the shit that rock 'n' roll takes you through and you get clean, sober, and start to recover from the disease, you really start to look at your life and say, "Thank you." When you're out there drinking and the whole bit, none of that "thankful" stuff matters. You don't even stop to think about it, so you can lose yourself very easily in thinking you're a god, and I say that from personal experience.

Touring with Down was a completely different experience than it was with Pantera, particularly outside of the U.S., and the reasons for that were that I was much more open to new experiences than I had been when I was younger and because some of the other guys, Pepper Keenan in particular, wanted to get out of the hotel to go and visit whatever's around that's worth seeing. I would never in a million years have wanted to go to Tel Aviv when I was in Pantera because I had preconceived (and inaccurate) notions of what it might be like. Don't judge a book by its cover, they say. Turns out Tel Aviv is not unlike walking down a beautiful American beach. Like walking down Santa Monica.

We cancelled the first time we got offered a chance to play there, but Pepper was so adamant we go that we took the next offer that came. The place we stayed at was nothing spectacular, but it was one block from the beach and I went surfing every day with Pepper. The surf was great, too, even though it almost killed me on the last day. There was an American restaurant and bar nearby, completely unexpected, right there on the boardwalk at the beach, and it was just perfect.

CHAPTER 22

SEVEN 'TIL SEVEN NO ONE KNOWS WHAT WILL HAPPEN

Despite being in a far different headspace than I'd been in for many years, I was still in a lot of pain in 2009 and 2010. I eventually couldn't take it anymore and went to my doctor and said, "Doc, something's really killing me. I'm in a lot of pain" and he jumped to an incorrect conclusion straight away by saying, "Well, Rex, you've got to quit drinking."

I told him the truth: "Dude, I haven't had a drink in over a year." So he goes, "Okay, let's get a CT scan then," but that didn't show up anything, and neither did the initial MRIs. Finally I got turned on to doctors at the United Methodist hospital in Dallas by some friends of mine who'd heard of a trial procedure that had yielded a very high success rate. During a 3D MRI scan they finally established that my pancreas was full of stones, or polyps if you want to be more medically precise.

The condition was called acute pancreatitis, and they told me that I also had some issues with my gall bladder and that it would have to be removed. It could have been the booze that caused all these issues, yes, but equally, this condition can occur in anyone between the ages of thirty-five and forty-five, and I was right on the upper edge of that category. And it can be fatal.

So they said to me, "Here's the way it's going to go. We'll try to get as many of these stones from your pancreas as we possibly can." So I went in about five times for non-invasive surgery. Then I got a rare form of ultrasonic treatment that blasted my stomach, again to try and dislodge some of these stones, but that didn't work either. What next?

We had been talking for a while about something called a Puestow procedure, in which they basically cut you in half; then they cut the pancreas in half, too, get all the stones out, and then you're good to go, except for the gaping hole in your fucking stomach. I was in the hospital for three weeks and I had a team of five looking after me around the clock while I got this relatively rare treatment.

When I got out of hospital after the treatment, I was only at the beginning of the rehabilitation process. I barely had a foot in the door. I still had to go back for regular check-ups, and during one of them they found that they'd sewn me up with a surgical stint still lodged in there. This uppity dude said, "Hey, I'm the one that sewed you up." And I'm like, "Great, but I've found out there's a band in there that you forgot to cut." So, I was in and out of there non-stop, pain after pain. I was taking a lot of fucking pain medication, and it wasn't helping at all. The years of abusing my system had finally caught up with me, and it was going to be a long process to reverse the effects. Worse still, it looked like I was going to have to learn to live with a considerable degree of pain as my punishment.

To deal with it, the doctors prescribed me oxycodone, which is an analgesic medicine derived from poppies, and it's very heavy-duty shit. But it does help with easing the pain.

The downside is that it also causes some side effects, and in my case the most common one was anxiety, something I'd been self-medicating for years as evidenced by my spiraling alcohol dependency. I was no longer advised to drink alcohol, so I continued taking Klonopin in order to combat the anxiety of not drinking, and the side effects caused by the pain meds. Sounds like a lot of medication, doesn't it? Well, it is and I really need to be careful. The penalties involved with any kind of alcohol relapse had been doubled after the pancreas surgery. Isn't it funny how life works.

TERRY GLAZE

Even when we were young—and maybe I shouldn't say this—I always thought that it would be Rex that went first because I thought his body would give out. Whether it would be his liver, a heart attack, or whatever; but not in a million years did I think it would be Darrell. We all have those people that we look at and say, "They are the one." And Rex was that guy within the band. The funny thing about Rex is that he remembers every fucking thing. *Everything.* I was talking to him the other day and I said to him, "Rex, didn't we play a show somewhere when Carmine Appice got up onstage with us?" He goes, "Yeah, it was Cardy's in Houston in 1984." "What song did we play?" and Rex immediately said, "Bark at the Moon" by Ozzy. And I said, "How the fuck do you *remember* that?" But that's typical of Rex.

I rejoined Down on the road for a while and we began the initial process of working out some ideas for a new bunch of songs. My life continued uneventfully, despite the occasional glitch on the road, and over time I recovered my strength. I was still dealing with chronic pain on a daily basis. It seemed like the regular medical services available only want to send you on a wild-goose chase in search of solutions. Pain management doctors are in cahoots with every other part of the chain it seems, so it's really hard to get definite answers on the best way to deal with the daily pain.

On the marriage front, Belinda and I had continual ups and downs, when we split up and got back together again, until we amicably separated in 2011 after we both agreed that it would be better for all concerned if we lived apart.

From a musical perspective, my life was also in transition. After a guest appearance on an Arms of the Sun record that appeared in 2011, and enjoying the process of playing a few live shows at places that we'd frequented during our club days, Philip Anselmo and I parted ways, maybe for the last time.

I left Down in 2011 for two reasons. First, I wanted a fresh start with another band to see where my musical journey would take me. Second, I was tired of dealing with some of the hypocrisy regarding lifestyle choices within the band. Philip and I had been working together for almost twenty-five years, and while we complement each other in many ways musically and will always be brothers in a spiritual sense, it was time for our paths to diverge, and for each of us to do our own thing away from the shadow of Pantera's legacy, while still carrying Darrell's spirit with us.

RITA HANEY

My line has softened over the years since Darrell's death, probably because I feel an element of forgiveness and a desire for everybody to get along. No matter what ever happened, nobody did this to Darrell. I mean they—Rex and Philip—didn't. The person who did it did it, and no matter what reason the killer—if he was still alive today—could give to justify that, it wouldn't change anything. But when you go through something like this, you want to lay blame somewhere. Obviously I had resentment to Rex and Philip because I had to watch Darrell trying to save his band. I wanted to fix it for him. As far as Philip is concerned, we are at least communicating, albeit on a fairly surface level. We haven't talked about any deep things like resentments because I've told him that I still harbor some resentment for how he handled band issues and how that impacted Darrell and I've made that very clear to him. And it's hard for me to trust him. But we'll see. It's a start and in time we'll probably sit down face to face.

Despite all the issues I'll say this: going out selling the merchandise for Darrell every summer has given me a whole different perspective. When you are with all the people that Pantera's music touched and you hear the stories they have about how a certain song got them through, even if they never got to see them, it makes you realize that you're being selfish and that your issues are petty and false. I'm not the big picture. *They* are. I'm so grateful for all the things I learned from Darrell and I want to try to be that kind of person you know. Better.

————

I love Philip as a brother like I always have; we still speak on the phone and have agreed not to talk publicly about each other's musical projects, and that's the best way our relationship can possibly be left. Despite a measure of disagreement on some levels, there will always be that mutual respect between us, and that will live forever. We went through everything together since we met as naive teenagers with the same drive to succeed, and that bond just cannot be broken by petty disagreement or a desire to mature in different directions.

RITA HANEY

I wish Vince was more like his brother when it comes to welcoming new people into his world, instead of feeling strapped up or that it's a problem or an inconvenience. Of course it can be overwhelming, I used to watch Darrell every day and marveled at how amazing he was at handling it, but I wish there was more of that in Vinnie. I know he has never really dealt with the death of his brother head on, and instead he's chosen to shut it away and hope that he'll never have to discuss it. If he was open to sharing some of his stories with people, he might just find peace, and if he let people in, he might also just see the big picture I'm talking about.

As for Vinnie Paul, who knows? We generally don't communicate and it's hard to know what will change that situation because he's extremely stubborn when he's made his mind up about something. As I've already said, I do feel empathy for him on a human level, and all I know is that I genuinely believe that if his brother Darrell was alive today, we would still all be playing together in Pantera. That was always my intention, and it's important to my brother Vinnie that he knows that ...

A WORD FROM THE AUTHOR

BARELY A DAY PASSES THAT I DON'T THINK ABOUT PANTERA. I dream about Pantera, have nightmares about Pantera—it's always there and I imagine it always will be. It's inevitable. After all, it was— and still is—a huge part of my life, despite ceasing to exist almost ten years ago. It might sound like a cliché, but we really were like brothers: me, Philip, Vinnie, and Dime. Unified from the beginning by a shared sense of how tough it was to be accepted in this business; as one, we lived and breathed every second of the wild ride that changed our lives in so many ways and came to a sickening, premature end one night in Columbus in 2004.

Along the way, as terrifying fame and huge piles of dollars start to fly at us from every fucking angle on the way to selling almost twenty million records across our major label career, our personalities changed—not always for the better either—and in doing so we began to want different things from that one precious shot at life that we were given. The problem was that while the albums and tours were grinding on relentlessly, we never got a chance to breathe, far less figure out who we were and where we really wanted to go, so instead of pulling us all together, the tension caused each of us to seek different, dark avenues of escape, which in turn drove us apart.

There were lots of valid reasons for writing this book and many sound arguments not to, but with the benefit of time and the critical perspective it brings, I felt that the real story of this band—at least from where I was standing—needed to be told. I intentionally never said much back then and in a many ways I'm glad I didn't because I know now that whatever had come out of my mouth would have been motivated by something other than simply an honest desire to tell my story as I lived it.

Instead I left the talking to the other guys, because that's just the kind of person I am. I'm the Silent Bob character in this whole scene, and while people look up to me, I don't really see myself that way— as famous—and I definitely don't need or want the attention. But being the buffer—the guy in the middle of warring factions—*was* draining and even if I'd wanted to, I just didn't have the energy to get involved in what quickly became a shit storm of accusations and counter-accusations.

I thought plenty, though, and after years of tight-lipped silence while dealing with my own personal Pantera aftermath, I gradually came to realize that in spite of everything negative that comes along, you have to be thankful for whatever is put in front of you in life, and only once you reach that point of realization can you even think about recounting the past with any semblance of clarity.

A NOTE FROM THE CO-AUTHOR

THE PHONE CALL THAT STARTED THE CONVERSATION ABOUT writing this book came at around 3 a.m. U.K. time. In fact, quite a few of Rex's calls came in the middle of what was my night. He'd been good enough to lend some interview material for a previous book of mine, and during that short process I felt that we formed a bond, despite being, in every sense, from two different worlds.

We talked at length about the process of telling the Pantera story from his point of view, and the well-known conflicts that had blighted the last few years of the band's existence. I soon learned that the gravity of the situation could not be underestimated and also that an honest account of what really happened would make for compelling reading.

Our conversations continued over the next year or so, some of that time being amid a few of the most challenging months of Rex's life, but throughout he was always forthcoming, usually in good spirits, and *never* late for a phone call or Skype session. That's just the kind of guy Rex is. He arranged for me to travel to Bucharest, Romania, in

May 2010, where Down was brought in to support AC/DC on short notice due to a cancellation by Heaven & Hell. That was the night we heard that Ronnie James Dio had died. Rex was devastated. Nothing else mattered to him that night because, as I said, that's the kind of guy he is.

Then I went to Northern Spain for a week with Down while they headlined a metal festival in Ribeiro, a place none of us had ever heard of, but the thousands of fans who descended on the place for the weekend obviously had directions. Rex and I stayed in a remote cottage in the woods—not unlike the cabin in *The Evil Dead*—and the plan was that we'd conduct the bulk of the interviews for this book, which we did over endless cups of tar-thick black coffee we just kept on reheating and refilling. To break the days up we drove around the little Spanish town incognito, in a rental van that had only one CD: *British Steel* by Judas Priest.

We also strengthened our connection, while I also gained an understanding of how the personal dynamics of Pantera worked, now that I was around two of the former members at close quarters. I learned a lot of things during that week, not least the sheer gravity and depth of the project I was involved with: the tensions, the resentment, the deep hypocrisy, and the not-so-easy life of a rock star ... I also discovered that the only item in the bedroom that would be my home for two long weeks was a large axe. I'm just glad I never had to use it on Rex!

ACKNOWLEDGMENTS

AS YOU'VE READ IN THIS BOOK, I'M NOT A SAINT, NOR HAVE I EVER
aspired to be one. I've simply tried to shine some perspective and insight onto my life so far, and the many beautiful people that have surrounded it. With all the trials and tribulations, sacrifices and tragedy, I'm very grateful for even having the chance to put a smile on the fans' faces. That's what it all boils down to after all, and it sure put a smile on my face.

When I was approached with the offer to write this book, I was somewhat skeptical. But after discussions with my friend Mark Eglinton, I thought that the time was right. I knew I was a little too young to write an epitaph, *ha-ha,* but this book isn't that at all. It's simply the account of a period in my life that I never previously explained fully in the press.

Particular thanks go to my co-writer Mark Eglinton, my agent Matthew Elblonk, my editor Ben Schafer, and all the in-house staff at Da Capo Press. I'd also like to offer special thanks to Christine Marra for project-managing the editorial production with the help of her excellent support staff: Jane Raese, Marco Pavia, and Jeff Georgeson. Your combined efforts resulted in a book I'm extremely proud of.

I'm truly in love with my kids. They are my salvation, my under-standing of this life, and two of the greatest kids that I've ever met. I think everybody says that about their kids, but these truly are two people that have been unscathed by what has gone on between the relationship, the moving outs, and all the crazy shit. I've omitted their names in this book for obvious reasons, but they are my end-all.

I've been blessed in many ways. I also believe that a higher power has always been present in my life, even though at times I didn't fully acknowledge it. I truly believe that God has somehow watched out for me. There's no other way to say it.

There are two people in the book that have affected me deeply: My ex-wife Belinda, who is not only a great mother to my children but also had to put up with my bullshit for all those eighteen years. The other is Elena, my first love. It's kind of unbelievable that we've reunited after all these years, and spending so much time together, it's as if we've never been apart. Even though we've matured in-tensely since those younger days. Without these two extraordinary women in my life, I don't think I could have dealt with everything that has come my way. I learned a lot of things through the years: struggle, the power within, patience and brotherly love that some-times in life can run cold. Especially with four egos melting into one ice-block disaster.

I've been blessed again, in the form of Vinnie Appice, my dear old friend and the baddest fucking drummer alive. Mark Zavon, my new right-hand man, as I used to call brother Dime. And the ever-fabulous Dewey Bragg. We all have a kinship for life like I remember from back in the old days of Pantera. The name of the band is Kill Devil Hill, and it has brought back the fire, the hunger, and the innocence I so desperately needed at a time that was crucial in my recovery from surgery and departure from Down. The future of this band is undeniable. We've worked our asses for almost two years and we're really making great strides for the future ahead. I haven't been this excited about jamming in a long time.

As for the legacy of Pantera, we'll keep rereleasing the old records, sometimes with a bonus track that will pop up with the weirdest and coolest timing. As far as Philip and Vince are concerned, Vinnie still carries around his hatred, and I'm not sure that will ever change. It's sad in every way imaginable, being that we used to be so tight in so many ways. Personally, I would love to give it one more shot, to not only play live, but to squash all the futile animosities that have thrown us so far apart. I want to give a big hug to Philip, Vinnie, Darrell R.I.P., and everyone else that we interviewed for this book.

About the only thing a man can sell out are his values. Something that he can never, ever get back.

Rex Brown, 2012

MY DEEPEST THANKS to my agent, Matthew Elblonk, who's always supremely calm under pressure; to Joel McIver; to both my families, especially my amazing sons, Andrew and Jack; and finally, to my fiancée, Linda Lee, without whom I don't know where I'd be.

Mark Eglinton

REX BROWN COMPLETE DISCOGRAPHY

Album Appearances

PANTERA
1983 *Metal Magic*
1984 *Projects in the Jungle*
1985 *I Am the Night*
1988 *Power Metal*
1990 *Cowboys from Hell*
1992 *Vulgar Display of Power*
1994 *Far Beyond Driven*
1996 *The Great Southern Trendkill*
1997 *Official Live: 101 Proof*
2000 *Reinventing the Steel*

COLLABORATIONS
1998 Jerry Cantrell, *Boggy Depot* ("Dickeye," "My Song," "Keep the Light On," "Satisfy," and "Hurt a Long Time")
2008 Cavalera Conspiracy, *Inflikted* ("Ultra-Violent")

DOWN
2002 *Down II: A Bustle in Your Hedgerow*
2007 *Down III: Over the Under*
2010 *Diary of a Mad Band: Europe in the Year of VI* (CD/DVD)

CROWBAR
2004 *Lifesblood for the Downtrodden*

DAVID ALLAN COE AND COWBOYS FROM HELL
2006 *Rebel Meets Rebel*

KILL DEVIL HILL
2012 *Kill Devil Hill*

ALSO BY MARK EGLINTON

James Hetfield: The Wolf at Metallica's Door

www.mark-eglinton.com